RUN A VOLUNTARY GROUP

£8.99

A guide to successful organisation and management

Chris Carling

How To Books

Cartoons by Mike Flanagan

British Library cataloguing-in-publication data
A catalogue record for this book is available from the British Library.

First published in 1995 by How To Books Ltd, Plymbridge House, Estover Road, Plymouth PL6 7PZ, United Kingdom. Tel: Plymouth (01752) 735251/ 695745. Fax: (01752) 695699. Telex: 45635.

Note: The material contained in this book is set out in good faith for general guidance and no liability can be accepted for loss or expense incurred as a result of relying in particular circumstances on statements made in the book. The law and regulations are complex and liable to change, and readers should check the current position with the relevant authorities before making personal arrangements.

Typeset by Concept Communications (Design & Print) Ltd, Crayford, Kent. Printed and bound by The Cromwell Press, Broughton Gifford, Melksham, Wiltshire.

Contents

List of Illustrations

Preface

Voluntary work does not consist of ladies of a certain age and class doing good works unto the lower orders . . . voluntary activity is a way to rebuild community from the bottom-up challenging the top-down approach which has done so much to alienate people from participating fully in their own communities.

Melanie Phillips, the Observer

Every year in the UK around 23 million adults do some form of voluntary work. Glance through any local newspaper, listen to any local radio station, and you will find groups asking for volunteers to plant trees, train as counsellors, sit on the end of telephone helplines or rattle collecting boxes in the street.

Less well known to the public is the hard slog that goes on behind the scenes to make all this voluntary activity possible. Large national charities usually have field workers whose job it is to support local branches. Some of the better funded local groups have at least part-time paid staff. But most community groups, at least in their early stages, have no one on the payroll. All the planning and organising, the fundraising and bill-paying, crisis-handling and general dogsbodying falls to committed volunteers.

If you are on the management committee of a local community group, or acting as an administrator/co-ordinator, or trying to get a new group off the ground, you have probably already found yourself plunged into areas you know hardly anything about, such as insurance, charitable status, giving interviews to the press or liaising with your local Council. This book will help you understand these and other key areas so you can make your group effective without having a nervous breakdown in the process.

It will show you how to:

- get your group properly organised from the start so that it runs smoothly rather than lurching from crisis to crisis;

- avoid some of the pitfalls and problems that can plague voluntary groups;

- make good use of all the specialised help available from national organisations such as the National Council for Voluntary Organisations and The Volunteer Centre UK – this is especially critical now that charities and voluntary groups are being encouraged to behave more like businesses in order to survive.

Last but not least, the book should help you keep a sense of perspective so that you do not get too bogged down in the nitty-gritty of running your group. If all that work is to be worthwhile you have to enjoy it and gain real satisfaction from seeing your organisation making its mark.

ACKNOWLEDGEMENTS

Many thanks to all those people involved with running voluntary groups who helped me write this book by talking freely about their experiences. Thanks too to the National Association of Volunteer Bureaux for permission to include the Volunteers Charter, to Glenda Rapaport for permission to reproduce the poster for attracting volunteers, and to the Charity Commission for permission to use their model constitution for an unincorporated association. Finally, a very special thanks to the staff of the Trustee Helpline at the National Council for Voluntary Organisations for patiently answering my many queries.

Chris Carling

IS THIS YOUR GROUP?

Befriending Scheme   Benefits Advice

                          Community Radio

Victim Support   Local History Group

                        Tenants Association

Community Centre   Play Scheme

                            AIDS Helpline

Hospital Friends   Sports Club

                      Bereavement Counselling

Community Mediation Service   Toy Library

                            Ethnic Forum

Women's Aid   Disabled Access Group

                            Church Group

Senior Citizens Club   Support Group for Single Parents

Conservation Volunteers   Rape Crisis Centre

                            Theatre Group

Youth Group   Self-help Group

                          Mobility Scheme

Photographic Club   Drugs Advice

                           Hospital Radio

Telephone Helpline   Playgroup

                       Mental Health Group

Residents Association   Local Rambling Club

                          Advocacy Scheme

Credit Union   Information Service

                           Pressure Group

IS THIS YOU?

Befriending Scheme Organiser   Self-help Group Co-ordinator

Tenants Association Chair

Theatre Group Leader   Volunteer Driver

Membership Secretary

Community Radio Organiser   Chair of Pressure Group

Residents Association Committee Member

Volunteer Co-ordinator   Conservation Volunteer –
                                                         Task Organiser

Chair of Support Group   Voluntary Group Treasurer
for Single Parents

Mobility Scheme Organiser

Playgroup Organiser   Executive Committee Member

Volunteer Advice Worker

Chair or Vice-Chair of a   Church Group Committee Member
Management Committee

Chair of Hospital Friends

Counselling Group Co-ordinator   Community Centre Organiser

Voluntary Group Office Administrator

Local History Group Chair   Disabled Access Group Organiser

Toy Library Organiser

Fund-Raiser   Voluntary Group Press Officer

Victim Support Co-ordinator

1
Setting Up

WHAT KIND OF GROUP?

No one knows exactly how many voluntary groups there are in the UK – the National Council for Voluntary Organisations' best guess is between 230,000 and 300,000. Nor is there any such thing as a typical voluntary group. Some are very small and specialised such as a local Swan Rescue Service or Brewery History Association or self-help group for sufferers from asthma or tinnitus. Some are branches of huge organisations – Age Concern, for example, has 1,400 branches with around a quarter of a million volunteers. Most fall somewhere in between.

All these different kinds of groups make different demands on the people who run them. Taking on too much is a common problem in the voluntary sector – you need to be realistic about the demands your group will make on your energy and time.

Here are three very different examples of voluntary groups. Compare the different demands made on their organisers:

Local history group
● Dennis is a retired builder and keen amateur historian who used an Open Day at his neighbourhood community centre to find like-minded people interested in setting up a local history group. Running the group makes modest demands on Dennis and his small committee. Their main responsibilities are:
  (i) booking premises and organising speakers for meetings;
  (ii) raising money to pay expenses from membership subscriptions.

Telephone helpline
● Nikki was one of a group of friends who were worried that people in their community who were HIV positive or suffering from full-

blown AIDS had nowhere to turn for support. They decided to try and ease the problem by setting up a telephone helpline. Though the idea seemed simple, the demands made on them as organisers were actually very high. They had to:

(i)   find premises;
(ii) recruit suitable volunteers to staff the helpline;
(iii) get these volunteers trained;
(iv) organise publicity – and that was all before the line was even open to the public.

Credit union

- A credit union is a kind of financial co-operative that takes in members' savings and lends them money at modest rates of interest. The law requires members of a credit union to have a common bond such as working for the same employer or belonging to the same association. A parents group linked to a local school decided to set up a credit union in their area. They found that running such an organisation makes major demands on organisers who have to:

(i)   understand fully the law governing credit unions;
(ii) accept a high degree of personal responsibility since the group is handling people's money. They also had to find premises as well as trying to raise money to employ staff to take in savings and pay out loans.

Now think about your own group. Does it make manageable demands on your time and energy as the local history group does on Dennis, or much greater demands on you and your co-organisers like the telephone helpline or credit union?

If your group is up and running, list everything you have done for the group in the last week noting down how long it took. Now do the same for the last month. Don't forget to add in all the worrying time when you weren't actually doing anything but still couldn't get the group and its problems out of your mind.

Does the amount of time the group takes up surprise you? Are you comfortable with this level of commitment or can you see a danger of the group taking over your life?

STARTING A NEW GROUP

The three groups discussed in the last section are very different. What they have in common is that they were all started by ordinary people

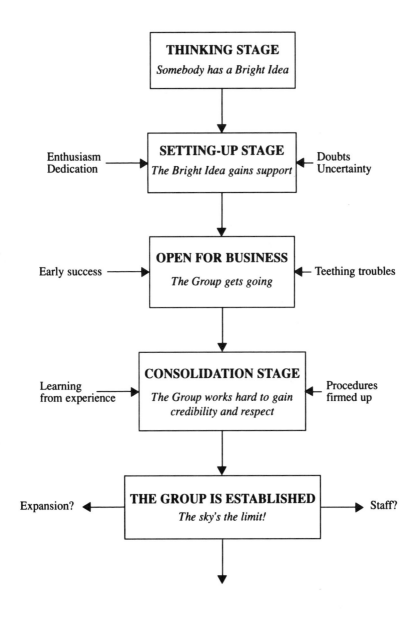

THINKING STAGE
Somebody has a Bright Idea

Enthusiasm
Dedication

SETTING-UP STAGE
The Bright Idea gains support

Doubts
Uncertainty

Early success

OPEN FOR BUSINESS
The Group gets going

Teething troubles

Learning
from experience

CONSOLIDATION STAGE
*The Group works hard to gain
credibility and respect*

Procedures
firmed up

Expansion?

THE GROUP IS ESTABLISHED
The sky's the limit!

Staff?

Fig. 1. Stages in the development of a group.

15

who got them going because they saw a need. All kinds of people set up and run voluntary groups – and most of them learn on the job.

Taking advantage of the early stages

Most groups go through a series of stages (see fig. 1). They start with a burst of enthusiasm followed by a buzz of activity as the group gets going. This gradually quietens into a consolidation phase before the group is finally established.

If your group is still in its early stages you have two big advantages:

- *Enthusiasm and commitment are high* – your job will be to keep people keen and interested in the face of the delays and setbacks you will almost certainly meet.

- *You are free to create the kind of organisation you want* – your group has no history until you invent it. You start with a clean sheet. To take advantage of all this freedom you and your co-organisers will have to put a lot of time and effort into hammering out how your organisation will be run.

It is also worth keeping in mind that the setting-up stage is special. It won't happen again. The skills you need for setting up may be quite different from those you need for managing the group once it is up and running. The people may be different too. Don't be too surprised if some of those heavily involved in setting up the group drop out and move on to something else. People who volunteer often have their own agenda which you do not always know about. See Chapter 3 for more on working with volunteers.

Two golden rules

These two rules apply to all voluntary groups at all stages of their development. If you can hang on to them your group will stand a much greater chance of running smoothly. The rules are:

- *Don't take anyone for granted.* Voluntary groups only work because a lot of people are prepared to give a lot of time, talent and energy for free. Some organisers forget this, particularly at hectic times when it is only too easy to trample on toes and make people feel taken for granted. A survey of volunteers reported that one in four felt their efforts were not always appreciated. You need to be extremely generous with praise and recognition – look on them as the fuel that keeps your organisation burning bright.

- *Don't take anything for granted.* This may sound boring and bureaucratic but it is crucial: you need to agree on a procedure for everything. Don't just say to your Treasurer: 'Right, you pay volunteers' expenses. . .'. Work out how this is to be done – decide which are valid expenses, design a simple claim form, work out a system for payment. The principle here is that it is much easier to set up a system at the start than to pick up the pieces later when things are falling apart.

CLARIFYING YOUR AIMS

'Make sure you have a clear idea of what your organisation exists to do' is the kind of good advice you may be tempted to dismiss as being far too obvious. Peter is the moving force behind a church group set up to organise a befriending scheme for the lonely and housebound. To him the point of the group seemed perfectly straightforward: their aim was to recruit volunteer visitors to befriend and visit lonely and housebound people in the parish.

But then Jean, one of the organising group, asked whether they would be visiting lonely people who were not housebound. But surely, said one of the others, the whole point of the scheme is to visit housebound people. Not necessarily, said another, there could be people who can get out but only with difficulty. But some of them aren't lonely, persisted Jean. I thought we were supposed to be cheering people up . . .

Don't be surprised if, like Peter, you find that your co-organisers have a variety of different ideas on why the group is necessary and what its priorities should be. Every group has basic issues that need to be clarified, preferably early on. Peter and his organising group were lucky – their differences came to light before they had really got going. They were able to clarify their aims and get the group off to a good start knowing they were all pulling in the same direction.

Asking the right questions
To help you clarify the aims of your group, discuss these questions with your co-organisers:

- Who precisely is your group aimed at?
- Does your group meet a need?
- How do you know this need exists?
- Are there other groups in your community doing something similar?

- If so, what are their aims and how is your group different?
- What is the single most important activity your group is involved in?
- If your group did not get off the ground what would be the result?

You will also find these questions useful even if your group is well established. Discussing them with your co-organisers should help unearth any differences that have developed and help get everyone back on the same course.

Putting it in writing

After discussing these questions you should find it much easier to work out and agree a simple statement summing up your organisation and setting out its aims. You need such a statement:

- *For yourselves* – to help make sure you are all working in the same direction.
- *To get support from others* – they need to know what you stand for and what you aim to do.
- *To apply for funding* – grant-giving bodies or sponsors will need a clear statement of your aims and some assurance that your group meets a genuine need.

Example – Homeworkers

This is a very simple example of the aims and objectives of a self-help group:

Homeworkers is a local network of people working from home. The group aims to:

- offer support to the growing number of people working at home both full-time and part-time;
- encourage professionalism among home-based workers;
- help home-based workers to promote their services and enjoy their independent status.

Now try drawing up a simple statement of the aims and objectives of your group. Don't leave all the work to one person. Get several of the key people in the group to put their ideas on paper then meet to pool the results.

GATHERING SUPPORT

If your group is to get off the ground you will need to gain support within your local community. You want to get people talking about you, put yourselves on the map. The time you spent earlier clarifying your aims should pay off at this stage. By now you and your co-organisers will each have the same clear idea as to why you exist and what you hope to achieve – which means that in public you will all be putting over the same positive message.

What kinds of support

Depending on your particular group you may be looking for different kinds of support. Most groups need at least:

- *Moral support* – which comes as people start to understand the aims of your group and spread the word, helping you build a positive image.

- *Practical support* – this may be help in kind such as rooms for meetings or the use of a photocopier. Or it may be in the form of advice and encouragement from, for example, a community worker or local councillor who may sit on your Steering Group.

- *Financial support* – hard cash may not be forthcoming immediately but by building up your local support you should improve your chances of getting funding in the longer term.

Who to talk to

You will find yourself doing a lot of talking at this stage as you try to convince as many influential people as possible that your group is worthwhile. These are some of the people you might want to contact:

- *Local councillors* – particularly important if you are likely to be applying for local authority funds.

- *Council officers* in departments relevant to the work of your group.

- *Members of other voluntary organisations* – to tap into their experience and help them see how your group's activities will fit in with theirs.

- *Professionals* such as health or social workers. Friendly, public-spirited solicitors and accountants are also very useful people to know.

- *Community workers* with responsibility for encouraging local groups.

- *Community organisations* such as your local Council for Voluntary Service, Rural Community Council or Community Health Council.

Note the names of all the people you have talked to so far. What was most positive and what was most negative about their response? Has anyone asked you questions you could not answer or raised issues you had not thought of? Can you answer these questions or discuss these issues if anyone raises them in the future?

Example – talking to the right people

One of the first moves of the organisers of the AIDS telephone helpline we discussed earlier was to approach the senior consultant in genito-urinary medicine at their local hospital for support. As a doctor treating AIDS patients he saw that the service would meet a genuine need and so paved the way for the group to get some initial funding from the local health authority. The group's links with the hospital also enabled them to get help from the Health Promotion Unit with training for their volunteers.

'It is extremely important for voluntary groups to make links with people inside the system,' says Nikki, who has been active in the group from the start. 'They know the funding routes and can help you find your way around. Of course you have to gain their respect – but once they can see you provide a good service they can be your biggest supporters in times of need.'

Tips for making effective contact

- *Make a list* – of all the people with power and influence who could help your group. Then decide how to approach them.

- *Start with people you know* – and build outwards. Ask supporters if you can use their names when contacting people they refer you to.

- *Follow up letters with phone calls* – you might find it easier to approach certain people in writing but try to build on this initial contact with a call.

- *Co-ordinate your efforts* – make sure you keep a record of who is contacting whom so you don't duplicate and make yourselves look inefficient.

- *Don't waste any offers of help* – build up an information bank of contacts you make (file cards will do). Note all offers of any kind – if you can't use the help now you may need it later.

HOLDING A PUBLIC MEETING

Some groups hold a public meeting at this stage. If you choose this route make sure you decide in advance what you want the meeting to achieve – you don't want people wandering off at the end not knowing what will happen next. A useful precaution is to ask everyone attending to sign in with their address and phone number so you can get hold of them again.

Once you have fixed a date for the meeting and booked the hall (and decided how to pay for it) you will need to consider:

- *Who to invite.* Which local councillors, representatives of local organisations, professionals and others with a special interest in the type of activity you are proposing? Should you try and get a local celebrity such as your MP to open the meeting?

ALLBURY DROP-IN CENTRE PROJECT
45 Exford Road, Allbury AL6 9PZ
01777-633233

PRESS RELEASE

5 May 199X

MP SUPPORTS PUBLIC MEETING TO PLAN
DROP-IN PROJECT

Local MP, Mr Jay Brown, will be the guest speaker at a public
meeting to be held on Tuesday, 8 May at 6.30 pm at the Allbury
Community Centre, 45, Exford Road, Allbury to discuss setting
up a drop-in centre for local unemployed people. Everyone interested is very welcome to attend.

The idea for the centre has come from unemployed people themselves who have formed a small organising committee backed by
local trade unions and churches.

'I wholeheartedly support this initiative,' says Mr Brown who has
attended some of the early meetings of the committee. 'There are
very few facilities for unemployed people here in Allbury. This
centre will fill a real need.'

For further information about the project or the meeting, contact
Alan Wright or Bridget Lennox on 01777-633233.

Fig. 2. Press release announcing a public meeting.

- *How to publicise the meeting.* As well as the people you invite you
  will want interested members of the public to attend. Send a press
  release announcing the meeting to the local newspaper and radio
  station (see fig. 2). Make simple posters and distribute them as
  widely as you can.

- *How to conduct the meeting.* You will need to decide the format of
  the meeting – will it be mainly discussion? Or will you have
  speakers followed by questions? How will you bring the meeting
  to a close? Will you serve refreshments? What will be the follow-
  up?

Meetings checklist

If you are running a public meeting you need to think about:

- *Aims* – what do you want the meeting to achieve?
- *Venue* – is it convenient? Is there enough parking space?
- *Time of day* – does it suit those people you hope will come?
- *Invitations* – have you missed anyone off your list?
- *Publicity* – how are people going to learn about the meeting?
- *Programme* – who will chair the meeting? What will be on the agenda?
- *Refreshments* – are there facilities for making tea/coffee? Will you charge? Will you serve them at the beginning or end?
- *Follow-up* – what will be your next step? Will you send notes of the meeting to everyone who attended?

Setting up a Steering Group

You might want to use the meeting to form a Steering Group to oversee the setting-up stage of your organisation. You probably already have an informal committee made up of the original organisers. This could be the moment to bring in some new blood by asking people at the meeting with ideas and experience to join you.

This could also be a good opportunity to constitute yourselves a little more formally. Appoint officers (Chair, Secretary, Treasurer) if you have not done so already. Set regular dates for Steering Group meetings and record discussions and decisions in formal minutes.

This extra formality is especially important if you are likely to be applying for charitable status or funding from public money. Even at this early stage you need to be seen as organised and competent.

EXAMINING YOUR OWN COMMITMENT

As your group starts to take off, you will be able to see more clearly how much work is involved. This is a good time to stand back and take a fresh look at your own commitment. Are you still as keen and enthusiastic as at the beginning? Or are doubts and disillusion starting to creep in?

Example – staggering under the load

Sally volunteered to act as the co-ordinator of a new group offering advice and support to young single mothers. There was no money to pay her but she was keen and willing and worked hard to get the group off the ground. But after a time: 'I realised that the more you do, the more people expect you to do. New volunteers coming in assumed I was a paid worker and that it was my job to get the service up and running.' When she tried to take more of a back seat the organisation began to fall apart.

Sally eventually withdrew having learnt her lesson: 'When a group is entirely run by volunteers you've got to share the load. I shouldn't have taken everything on my shoulders. I should have made it clear much earlier that I was a volunteer just like everybody else.'

Being honest with yourself

Use these questions to help you think through your own feelings about the group at the moment:

- Why did I join the group?
- What did I want to get out of it?
- What have I got out of my involvement so far?
- Do I feel comfortable in the group? If so, why? If not, why not?
- Are there people I really like/dislike working with? If so, who? Why?
- Do I feel under pressure? Are people expecting more commitment from me than I want to give?

Some warning signs

Many groups work well and achieve a lot with few resources. But some lurch from crisis to crisis causing havoc in the lives of those trying to keep them afloat. These are some of the warning signs that things are going badly wrong:

- *Deep disagreements between key people.* One community theatre group was split on ideological grounds – some believed passionately that anyone in the community who wanted to should be able to take part in their productions regardless of talent, others believed equally passionately that they should be very selective and aim for professional standards.

- *Organisers are unreliable.* Promising the earth but usually failing to deliver.

- *Little lasting support for the group.* New recruits soon get disillusioned and drift away.

DRAWING UP A CONSTITUTION

Sooner rather than later, your group will need to draw up a constitution laying out the rules by which you will run your affairs. A formal, written constitution is necessary:

- *For yourselves* – so everyone involved is clear how the group operates and how decisions are made.
- *For the outside world* – to give confidence to possible funders and other supporters who will be able to see you are a properly constituted, well-managed and accountable group with clear lines of responsibility.

Your group's constitution is what is known as its 'governing document' which needs to be thought through and carefully worded. It is worthwhile getting a solicitor or other legal expert to help in drawing up your constitution, or at least to check it through. Legal advice is vital if you expect to apply for charitable status since the Charity Commission will scrutinise your constitution very closely.

Many groups do apply for charitable status. In fact, some funders will only give money to registered charities. If you know you are going to apply then you should draw up a draft constitution and submit it to the Charity Commission before it is formally approved. Chapter 8 gives more details on becoming a charity as well as on legal structure. (Note than a constitution is not the only kind of governing document. If your group is a charitable trust your governing document would normally be a trust deed. If you become a company limited by guarantee you will be governed by a Memorandum and Articles of Association.)

Getting help

If drawing up a constitution sounds difficult it needn't be. Plenty of groups have been there already and you should take advantage of all the help and guidance around. Start by getting hold of a specimen constitution. The National Council for Voluntary Organisations can provide examples, while for groups applying for charitable status the Charity Commission has produced a set of model governing documents (see Appendix).

Talk to other local groups and have a look at their constitutions – if you are a local branch of a national organisation consult your headquarters. Can you think of anyone locally who might be knowledgeable about the ins and outs of constitutions? Approach them and ask for advice.

What to include

Though the details will depend on your particular group, your constitution would normally cover at least the following areas:

- *The full name of your group.*

- *Objects.* Here you would give a clear statement of what your group exists to do. Note that this is a very important section if you will be applying for charitable status since your objectives need to fall within the Charity Commission's definition of a charity. Always seek advice.

- *Powers.* What you intend to do to achieve your aims.

- *Membership.* You would probably want to spell out who may join your group and on what terms. Will you have different classes of membership such as individual, group, honorary? Do you need a section on subscriptions?

- *Management committees.* Here you would lay out the management structure of your group. Most groups are run on a day-to-day basis by a management or executive committee often with sub-committees dealing with specific areas such as finance or training. In this section you would include details such as the size of the committee, who would be eligible for membership and how long they could serve.

- *Elections.* How are the members of your management committee to be appointed? Will you want to co-opt members? If so, how many? For a new group you may wish to include a clause on how the first committee will be set up.

- *Officers.* The officers you need (normally at least Chair, Secretary, Treasurer) and how they are to be appointed.

- *Meetings.* How often your management committee and any other committees should meet and how meetings should be conducted, including the minimum number of members that must be present to make a quorum. You will probably also want to include details of the Annual General Meeting.

- *Accounts*. Details of what the group's funds may be used for, how the accounts are to be kept and arrangements for auditing.

- *Winding up*. What would the procedure be for winding up the group and who may set this in motion.

- *Altering the constitution*. What would be required to alter any part of the constitution.

Tips for drawing up your constitution

- *Use all available expertise*. Find out who has the necessary know-how and ask them to help. Try and identify the main pitfalls to avoid.

- *Look ahead*. Think about ways the group might develop, such as needing to employ staff or buy equipment. Try and keep the wording particularly of your objectives broad enough to allow for future development.

- *Test drive your draft*. One important role of a constitution is to settle disagreements. Try and imagine possible situations that may arise in the future and see whether your constitution would cover them.

IDENTIFYING SOURCES OF FUNDING

Money is nearly always an issue for voluntary groups. Exceptions are special interest groups such as Dennis's local history group or some self-help groups that cost little to run and can raise all they need from their members. Don't be surprised if some of your co-organisers have a blind spot about money. Some people are frightened by finance and in some groups the post of Treasurer is a difficult one to fill.

In the early stages you will need to think about two questions:

How much do we need to get started?

- Can you start small like Peter who ran his befriending service from a spare bedroom in the early days producing publicity on borrowed equipment? Starting small can give you time to prove yourselves and get over any teething troubles before taking on commitments such as premises or staff. If cash is crucial from the start because you need to train volunteers or rent premises or buy equipment you cannot borrow, raising money will have to be an urgent priority.

How much do we need to operate for the first year?

● To find out you need to start putting together a budget, that is, a list of what you need to spend money on and how much. (See Chapter 5 for advice on managing money.) If your needs are modest you may be able to raise enough from fund-raising events. But if you have significant expenses such as rent to pay, you will probably have to look for outside funding.

To get a rough idea of how much you need to run your group, do a quick, back-of-an-envelope budget. Write down everything you absolutely must spend money on in the year to come – phone, stationery, volunteers' expenses, insurance, rent maybe – and an estimate of how much. Total it all up. Now think about where you are going to get that kind of money.

Some sources of cash

Looking for funding is hard work and time-consuming. Finding it shows that someone out there is taking you seriously – which can give your group a real boost. These are some of the main sources of funds for voluntary groups:

● *Members and supporters* – for example, subscriptions and donations. Established groups sometimes receive legacies.

● *Grant-giving bodies* – such as charitable trusts and foundations, local authorities, central government. Many groups are supported in this way especially those providing a service to the community. But the picture is changing rapidly with more demands now made on groups to show they are giving value for money. The trend is for local authorities to move from straight grants to some form of contract.

● *Sponsorship* – many businesses sponsor voluntary groups and some companies have large sponsorship programmes. The bad news is that they all receive huge numbers of applications.

● *Fund-raising events* – from jumble sales to sponsored parachute jumps. These are an excellent use of volunteers' time if the main point of your group is to raise money for a particular cause. But they are not always such a good idea for groups trying to cover their running costs. Organising fund-raising events can take up a lot of time and divert energy from the main activities of the group.

Tips for keeping on a firm financial footing

● *Be realistic*. Don't underestimate what your group will cost to run.

● *Be imaginative*. Think about all the ways you can get help in kind – could you pay for printing, for example, by including advertising in your leaflets?

● *Be prepared* – for anything to do with money to take up more of your time than you ever thought possible.

FINDING PREMISES

What is your address?

Your group may not need its own premises straightaway but you will need an address. If you are running your group from home, think carefully about whether you are prepared for your address to be used on the group's headed paper and publicity material. Find out how the other members of your household feel. If there are problems, consider using a box number or persuade a friendly group with an office to let you use their address.

Example – running a group from home

Jackie runs a local victim support scheme from her home. She is a full-time paid co-ordinator managing a large caseload and fifty volunteers. For her, running the group from home is possible because she has made a deliberate effort to keep her work and private life separate. The group has its own phone line with an answering machine so Jackie does not have to take calls outside working hours. None of the publicity material for the scheme gives her address. She also has an office away from the rest of the house: 'If you're going to run a group from home, you need a whole room devoted to it. If you have to clear everything away to free the space it can't really work.'

Keeping costs down

For some groups finding suitable premises is a central issue. But for many others premises simply means a base, a tiny office with a desk, a phone and a hand-me-down filing cabinet.

Having your own base has advantages – it can give your group credibility as well as providing a place for volunteers to get together and people using your service to call. The disadvantage is that even a small office costs money. To keep costs down you can:

- See if you can negotiate an office rent-free – one community radio group got studio space in a local college; the AIDS helpline got their first premises at a peppercorn rent from their local health authority.

- Check whether your local Council, Council for Voluntary Service or other community group has low-cost units for rent to voluntary groups.

- Share with one or more other groups.

MAKING THE MOST OF VOLUNTEERS

Once your group is up and running you will have a good idea how many volunteers you need to operate effectively and what you want them to do. In the early stages you may not be so sure. Though Jackie's victim support scheme now has fifty volunteers, they only had a handful in the early days.

The number of volunteers you need to run a service such as a be-friending scheme will depend on the number of people needing the service. These numbers will take time to build up. If you attract too many volunteers too early and there is hardly anything for them to do, they may well have lost interest by the time you actually need them.

In the early stages you will need to consider the following:

- *How many volunteers do you need?* Do you need them all at once or only occasionally, for example, for fund-raising? Do you need them mainly to run the organisation or to provide the service your group offers to the community – or both? Can you start with a small number of volunteers and build up from there?

- *What kind of people are you looking for?* What do you need people to do and what qualities or skills, ideally, should they have?

- *Do they need training?* If so, how are you going to organise the training? Are there sympathetic organisations that might help?

See Chapter 3 for more on recruiting and managing volunteers.

CHECKLIST

Setting up a voluntary group is a lot of work. You cannot expect to do everything at once. Work within your limits and don't feel guilty about not doing more. To recap, the key areas to think about are:

- *Demands on your time and energy* – can you cope?

- *Aims and objectives* – are you clear about what your group exists to do?

- *Support* – who are your natural supporters? How can you get them on your side?

- *Steering Group* – have you enough support to form an effective Steering Group?

- *Constitution* – are you far enough ahead to draft a constitution?

- *Money* – how much do you need and where is it going to come from?

- *Premises* – do you need an office or other premises?

- *Volunteers* – how will you use volunteers at the start? How will you give them training and support?

TALKING POINTS

- You and your co-organisers are friends who have been meeting informally at your house, sometimes late into the night. After a public meeting you now have a more formal Steering Group with new members. Can you think of any problems that might now arise?

- You and your co-organisers are working hard drafting your constitution and putting in grant applications for funding. Suddenly a key person announces she has had enough – all this paperwork and bureaucracy was not what she joined the group for. She is leaving. What would you say to her?

- How would you feel about running your group from home?

2
How to Get Things Done

WHY YOU NEED A MANAGEMENT COMMITTEE

One of the aims of this book is to help you get your group on to a firm footing so that you are all clear about who does what and how decisions are made. To get there you need an effective management committee.

'Management committee' is a term widely used to refer to the people in overall charge of a voluntary group with legal responsibility for what it does and the decisions it takes. Many groups call their 'management committee' by another name such as the Executive Committee, the Steering Committee, the Management Board, the General Council or just the committee.

In the early days you and your co-organisers may not even think of yourselves as a committee at all. 'We were all friends – we used to meet in each others' houses,' says Tessa who helped set up a support group for victims of rape. 'It was when we started applying for charitable status we realised we were going to have to tighten up on the way we did things.' In some groups getting together informally works for a time. But once you start recruiting volunteers or handling sizeable sums of money – and certainly if you want to apply for charitable status – you need a more formal structure.

A properly constituted committee gives you a framework for running your group so you don't have to reinvent yourselves every time you meet. You need a management committee to make sure your group:

- makes decisions openly after proper discussion;

- is seen to be accountable to members, funders, supporters and users;

- handles money in a responsible manner;

- is outward-looking and willing to involve new people with relevant experience and expertise.

WHO SHOULD BE ON YOUR MANAGEMENT COMMITTEE

Volunteers sought
Carecom, a city-based charity which raises funds for the visually impaired and the physically disabled, is seeking volunteers to serve on its management committee.

(Short news item in a local paper)

Groups can sometimes find it hard to persuade people to serve on their management committee. 'I approached a friend I was sure would be sympathetic, but he said, no, absolutely not. I was very surprised,' says Bob who chairs a group that collects unwanted items of furniture and passes them on to people who need them.

One effect of the latest Charities Acts has been to make members of management committees more aware of their responsibilities and this may have made some people more wary of agreeing to serve. Fortunately, many others still remain willing. Though there are no really reliable figures, one recent estimate suggests the number of people serving on the management committees of voluntary groups may be close to the three million mark.

How big a committee do you need?
Your constitution should lay down the number of people on your management committee including how many you may co-opt and how many you need to make a quorum. Some groups have huge committees – thirty or more members is not unknown. Though there are no hard and fast rules, a committee smaller than about six risks becoming a clique, while one bigger than twelve to fifteen could be cumbersome to manage.

Who do you need?
The kind of people you need on your committee will depend partly on the stage you are in your development. In the early days when you have no money for paid staff, members of the management committee will have to take an active part in the day-to-day running of the group. At this stage you need mainly doers, hands-on people willing to get on and do whatever it takes to get the group up and running.

Later, when you are well enough established to have paid staff, the management committee will be less concerned with the day-to-day running of the group and more with supervising and policy-making. At this stage, if you can get them, you need people with ideas, thinkers, planners with a vision of the group's future.

Getting a good mix

Whatever stage you are at you should try and find people with different views representing different sections of your local community. Recent research has shown that most management committees at the moment have few young or black or disabled or working-class people among their members.

Though there is no such thing as a typical management committee, many have a mix of three kinds of people:

- *Active volunteers* – people with the necessary time and commitment to turn decisions into action. Such people are crucial in groups with no paid workers.

- *Interested professionals* – people working within the system who can be useful to your group; for example, community workers for a group trying to set up a community centre. Many groups have representatives of funding bodies or other relevant agencies. Victim support schemes, for example, have representatives from the police and the probation service on their committees.

- *Key supporters* – people with influence in your community such as local councillors or business people or key figures in other voluntary groups. These are essentially people who can help raise your profile and improve the chances of your group finding financial or other forms of support.

The great and the good

Getting powerful people involved in your group can be a big plus if they are committed and prepared to be active. If they are willing to lend their names to your cause but not do much more, you may be better asking them to be patrons of your organisation rather than inviting them on to your management committee. A star-studded committee is fine so long as you don't end up with too many chiefs and not enough indians. You need to keep in mind that in the end someone has to do the actual, mundane, day-to-day work.

Example – dealing with dead wood

Sometimes people agree to serve on a management committee then do nothing. You can't afford to carry people like these. Bob ran into the problem of dead wood when he took over as Chair of the group collecting unwanted furniture. Many different agencies referred people needing furniture to the service and one of the original organisers had invited a number of these agencies to be represented on the committee. By the time Bob took over, most of these representatives had stopped turning up for meetings. He had not even met some of them – they were just names on a list. The people who did turn up were the active volunteers – the ones who were running the group day-to-day. By writing and phoning Bob tried with limited success to get the no-shows to clarify their position. The group is now in the process of rethinking the composition of the management committee so that it better meets their needs.

Seeking commitment
You could, as some groups do, build in to your constitution a requirement that members of the management committee must attend a minimum number of meetings in a year. That way you have grounds for politely asking non-attenders to leave.

If you already have a committee
Write down the names of all the members. Beside each name note their main contribution to the committee – it could be some special skill but equally it might be some aspect of their personality such as straight talking or infectious enthusiasm. Have you got a good mix? What other kinds of people would it be useful to add?

UNDERSTANDING YOUR RESPONSIBILITIES

People often drift into becoming members of a management committee. Bob got involved when one of the original organisers asked if he could help out with the group for a few hours a week. 'Not long afterwards this chap left the area and I found myself practically running things.'

Groups often don't make it at all clear to management committee members the kind of responsibility they are taking on. Many voluntary groups, particularly in their early stages, are what are known as 'unincorporated associations' (as opposed to incorporated associations which are mainly companies). In law an unincorporated association is seen simply as a collection of individuals. The people running the group – normally the management committee but it could be all the members – may be held personally responsible if things go wrong.

Members of management committees are sometimes surprised, even shocked, to learn that they may be personally liable if, for example, money is mishandled or the group gets into debt. In practice, however, most people serving on the committees of 'unincorporated associations' emerge unscathed. Knowing you could be personally liable if things get in a mess is a strong incentive to act responsibly and make sure others do the same. Some groups now take out trustee liability insurance which can give some protection to management committee members of groups which are registered charities. See Chapter 4 for details.

Main responsibilities

The simple answer to the question of what the management committee is responsible for is – everything. This does not mean members of the committee necessarily have to do everything. But they are responsible for seeing that everything gets done.

What 'everything' means in practice depends on the kind of group. The main areas most committees need to be concerned with include:

- *Policy-making and planning.* What are the aims of the group? Not just today but in the longer term? Groups often get bogged down in the day-to-day but you also need to look ahead. What should you be doing to achieve your aims? How can you monitor progress?

- *Accountability.* Is your group being run democratically? According to your constitution? Is it clear who is responsible for what and how decisions should be made?

- *Financial affairs.* Does your group have an effective system for running its finances? Can you meet all your financial obligations?

- *Legal obligations.* Particularly in areas such as financial record-keeping, insurance, equal opportunities, health and safety, Data Protection Act, tenancy agreements or leases if you rent premises, employment contracts and employment law if you employ staff.

Registered charities

In the eyes of the law a charity's trustees are the people responsible for its general control and management – in other words, the management committee. If your group is a registered charity the members of your management committee will be the charity trustees. This is the case whether you actually call yourselves trustees or not.

Charities are answerable to the Charity Commission which lays down requirements concerned with accounts, reporting and other duties. See Chapter 8 for more information on becoming a charity as well as on the different legal structures your group may take.

Being prepared to answer questions

Anyone you ask to serve on your management committee will need information about your group if they are to commit themselves. These are some of the questions you should be prepared to answer:

- What does the group do?
- What are its main priorities?
- Who else is involved?
- What is the group's financial position?
- How much time will I be expected to give?
- How often are meetings held? At what time of day?
- How long will they normally last?
- What will be expected of me outside meetings?
- Why me? What do you expect me to contribute?

Tips for serving members

If you are serving on a management committee:

- *Master the constitution.* Many people never read their group's constitution. You need to be familiar with it so you know how the group should be run.

- *Don't be afraid to ask basic questions.* Make sure you understand everything. Don't agree to anything you are unclear or uneasy about.

- *Don't be steamrollered.* If you foresee problems with a course of action insist on bringing the difficulties into the open. If your funding is not secure, for example, your group needs to consider very carefully before taking on long-term commitments such as leases on buildings or even for office equipment such as photocopiers. Groups have occasionally run into difficulties when their grants have been suddenly cut and they have been left with leases with years to run and no money to pay.

SETTING UP THE COMMITTEE

In some groups the management committee has a life of its own evolving and changing as people drop out and new members are invited on by those already serving. Many community-based groups are more democratic. Such groups often have a membership structure with members electing the management committee and some or all of the officers at the Annual General Meeting.

In practice, electing the committee often means members agreeing that those people nominated shall be elected. Only if you receive more than one nomination for an office or more nominations than places on the committee will you need to hold an actual ballot.

If you are responsible for organising the election of the management committee of your organisation:

- Read the constitution – if it lays down a procedure for electing the committee, follow it faithfully.

- Allow plenty of time for people to send in nominations.

- Make sure the instructions on the nomination papers are clear – for example, can people nominate themselves? Do they need to get the agreement of people they nominate?

- If you have to hold a ballot, make sure the election is seen to be fair and open.

ELECTING OFFICERS

Your committee will need at least a Chair, Secretary, Treasurer and possibly Vice-Chair, elected either at the Annual General Meeting or by the other committee members. Though most people have a broad idea what the Chair, Secretary and Treasurer of a committee do, you still need to spell out their roles for your particular group. This is particularly important if you employ staff. Much of the work that might otherwise fall to the Secretary, for example, may be done by a staff member if such a person exists.

Some important 'don'ts'

If you want your committee to be effective:

- *Don't push people into jobs they don't really want.* They won't do them well and the whole group will suffer. Encourage people to take on offices by all means but learn to recognise when people are sincerely saying no.

- *Don't re-elect an officer, who has not been doing the job well.* This may seem obvious but in some groups members are only too pleased when someone is willing to take on a job however badly they do it.

- *Don't let officers carry on too long.* The Chair of a committee is not a job for life. Your constitution should set limits on the length of time officers can serve.

Taking the Chair

The Chair of any committee is a key figure responsible not just for planning and running meetings but also for keeping the group on track, making sure it sticks to its policies and gets its priorities right. Everyone can think of lots of qualities a Chair should have – dynamism, leadership, commitment, dedication, plenty of useful personal contacts – but it is important to remember that:

- *People can grow into their roles.* Look around at some of the people who don't push themselves forward. They may well have talents ripe for development. 'I never thought I was the kind of person that could stand up in public,' says Jenny who was talked into becoming Chair of her local tenants association. 'But once I'd spoken up a few times I really started to enjoy it. I look on it as a challenge now – getting things done.'

- *You may well be better off with a slightly less dynamic person* with real dedication and commitment to the group than a more obvious choice with too many other irons in the fire.

The Secretary

Try and find someone temperamentally suited to the role of Secretary, someone who really cares about detail who will unfailingly make sure the room is booked for meetings and agendas are sent round on time, someone who thinks it is important to get the wording of minutes or a letter just right.

The Treasurer

Most people who can do simple arithmetic can learn to be a Treasurer – you don't need to be an accounting wizard. Try and find someone with a responsible, law-abiding streak. You need to be able to rely on your

Treasurer to keep the books competently, pay bills on time and warn the committee well in advance of any possible financial problems.

Bear in mind that someone who would make a good Treasurer is not necessarily the kind of dynamic, outgoing person you need for fund-raising. Many groups separate these two areas – though it is important that your Treasurer and fund-raising expert get on and can work together.

Your group?
Think about the officers in your group. Jot down a list of the main jobs each of them is responsible for. Do you think you've got the right people for each job?

GETTING OFF TO A GOOD START

'When I first started going to meetings, I wondered what I was doing there. Two or three people did practically all the talking. Nobody explained what anything was about so there wasn't much I could say,' reports Ellen, who joined the management committee of a group working with children with disabilities.

Like Ellen many people serving on management committees are thrown in at the deep end. Nobody really tells them what is going on. They normally assume everyone else is clear about what the committee is trying to achieve, though this may be an illusion. Some committee members remain hazy about what is expected of them for months, if not years, reluctant to ask basic questions.

A good way to get your management committee working well as a team is to organise a training session. This is a particularly good idea if the people on your committee do not really know each other. You can use the session to:

● *Help them get to know each other better* – and start seeing themselves as a team.

● *Develop some broad aims for the year ahead* – don't decide these in advance. Let the committee work together to produce them.

● *Make members aware of the role and responsibilities of the committee* – give everyone a copy of the constitution. Make it clear how they can get issues they care about on to the agenda for meetings.

Ideally you should try to hold this kind of session whenever a new committee takes over the running of the group. You can either bring in a trainer experienced in team building, or plan and run the session yourselves.

Example – building a team

The management committee of one community group spent a Sunday afternoon together a few months after they were elected discussing the group and where it was going. Members were encouraged to be frank and honest and bring niggles into the open. Each person was given space to talk about themselves and their lives, what they had done in the past and what they felt they could offer. Everyone learnt something about others they hadn't known before and most of the committee went home with a renewed sense of commitment.

RUNNING MANAGEMENT COMMITTEE MEETINGS

People have written whole books on how to run meetings effectively. Few people seem to gave read them, though, judging by the way meetings are conducted in many groups. The trouble with meetings is that no one really wants to be there all that much. None of your team wakes up in the morning and thinks 'Great! I've got a management committee meeting this evening', which means you have resistance to get over before you even start.

Problems with meetings

It helps if you are aware of some of the pitfalls so you can try and avoid them. Two of the most common are:

- *Meetings that drag on too long* – because the agenda is too long, or discussions are allowed to go off at a tangent.

- *Meetings that never seem to get anywhere* – because no decisions are taken or if they are, no one ever seems to turn them into action.

Do your meetings suffer from either or both of these problems? If so, what do you think are the reasons?

Three stages of a meeting

To improve your chances of running meetings well you need to view each meeting as having three distinct stages: before, during and after.

ALLBURY COMMUNITY GROUP

The next meeting of the Executive Committee of the Allbury Community Group will be held on Tuesday, 15th May at 7.30 pm in the main meeting room. This is our last meeting before the AGM – it is important for everyone to be there.

AGENDA

1. Chair's opening remarks

2. Apologies for absence

3. Minutes of last meeting

4. Matters arising not elsewhere on the agenda
     (1) Trampoline repairs
     (2) Health and safety workshop

5. Treasurer's report

6. Annual General Meeting – finalising arrangements

7. Drop-in Centre Project – progress report enclosed

8. Publicity committee – proposals for membership drive

9. Any other business

10. Date of next meeting

Fig. 3. Agenda for a management committee meeting.

Before the meeting

You need to plan – starting with the agenda (see fig. 3). The agenda is a key document which needs to be drawn up well in advance, particularly if you want to send it out with discussion papers or other documents. Ten days to a fortnight before the meeting is comfortable, though the officers of many groups live dangerously and wait until just a few days before. In one group members hardly ever got their papers before the morning of the meeting – which meant they never had time to read them and were never prepared.

When planning your agenda:

- *Be realistic.* Don't try and crowd in more items than you can comfortably deal with in about an hour and a half. Easier said than done unfortunately.

- *Get your priorities clear.* Every meeting has one or two key items which should be the main meat of the discussion. Decide which these are and allow time to do them justice. Put short business items early to get them out of the way and leave time for more complex issues.

- *Think through each item in advance.* Talk through the point of each item with the Secretary and/or Vice-Chair including how you will handle it and what you hope to achieve. If you want someone else to introduce an item, let them know in advance.

Look back at the agenda of your last meeting in the light of the way things actually went. With hindsight would you make any changes to the agenda?

On the day

The role of the person in the chair is to guide and control the meeting. To do this effectively you need to:

- *Keep things moving.* Some meetings spend far too long on the early, less important items. Try and reach the key items as rapidly as you can. But be tactful – the Chair of one group prided himself in being brisk and getting through the agenda but many of the committee found him brusque and resented the way he kept rushing things on.

- *Stick to the agenda.* Don't let your meeting be side-tracked. If someone raises a major issue not strictly on the agenda propose a way of dealing with it – perhaps as an agenda item at the next meeting – and move on.

- *Take the lead but don't dominate.* Guiding and controlling the meeting does not mean doing most of the talking. Your role is to pull the discussion together and help focus on key issues. Everyone needs to feel they have the chance to have their say.

- *Sum up what has been agreed at the end of each item.* People need to feel that there has been a point to each item and that something has been achieved.

- *Make sure decisions are agreed formally and recorded.* Don't leave room for doubt or misunderstanding. Repeat what has been agreed so that the Secretary can take it down accurately for the minutes.

After the meeting
- *Think over how things went.* Was it a good meeting? If so, why? If not, what went wrong? Did you achieve what you hoped? Did everyone speak?

- *What needs to be followed up?* Who has agreed to do what? By when? Will they need chasing up? By whom?

- *Start thinking about the next meeting.*

Most committees have some members who rarely say anything. Who are the silent ones on your committee? How could you get them to play a more active part?

Example – the role of observers
In the interests of openness and democracy, groups with a membership structure sometimes say that any member can attend management committee meetings as an observer. One local community-based group positively encouraged members to attend. Observers could speak freely at the monthly committee meetings of this group. An outsider would not have been able to tell who was on the committee and who was not.

Nor, as it turned out, could new members of the group. Encouraged to attend the meetings, they often did not understand their observer status and sometimes voted – only to be told by the Chair that they were not entitled to vote. This confusion was bad for the group giving rise to ill feeling.

Avoiding the problem
If your group allows members to attend management committee meetings as observers it is important to make sure they understand their status. Normally observers are only allowed to speak if invited by the Chair. If you want members not on the management committee to have the chance to air their views, call a general meeting. Here everyone will have the same status and can speak freely.

CLARIFYING WHAT NEEDS DOING

The report of a recent working party looking at ways of increasing the effectiveness of management committees suggested that some committee members are reluctant to offer a firm direction to their group. They agree to serve because they are interested in the work of the group – not because they want to manage.

Sally, the volunteer who acted as unpaid co-ordinator of the group offering support to young mothers, would endorse this view. When she had problems, feeling she was carrying too much of a load, she turned to the Chair of the management committee for help and found only well-meaning vagueness.

It may have been that the Chair simply did not know what to suggest. People in key positions in voluntary groups are suddenly supposed to know how to manage whether or not they have ever done so before.

The second golden rule
If your management committee is short on experience you can normally stay on the straight and narrow by going back to the second golden rule:

● **Don't take anything for granted**

Be as explicit as you can about as much as you can. In many groups, for example, the question of who has the authority to do what is not made clear. Often this only comes to light when things go wrong and someone spends money in ways others are not happy about or speaks to the press about matters which should have been confidential. You can avoid these kinds of problems by deciding as a matter of policy who should be able to speak for the organisation. Should it be the Chair, or any one of the officers, or a specially designated publicity officer? It doesn't matter so much *what* you decide as *that* you decide on a policy on which everyone agrees.

Setting up sub-committees

Many groups set up sub-committees to deal with key areas such as finance, training, administration and publicity. This is a good way of spreading the load but here again – don't take anything for granted. The management committee needs to approve the membership of any sub-committees and provide a clear remit so that those serving will know what is expected of them (see fig. 4). Members of sub-committees need

---

ALLBURY COMMUNITY GROUP

Finance Sub-Committee Remit

Overall aim:
To oversee the financial management of the Allbury Community Group on behalf of the Executive Committee.

Main Responsibilities:

- Prepare annual draft budget for discussion and approval by the Executive Committee

- Prepare annual accounts for approval by the Executive Committee and liaise with auditors

- Monitor income and expenditure of the Allbury Community Group checking that spending is in line with the budget agreed by the Executive Committee

- Report current financial position to the monthly meeting of the Executive Committee

- Advise on financial feasibility of new initiatives

- Look for opportunities to increase the income of the Allbury Community Group

---

Fig. 4. Example of a sub-committee remit.

to understand that they do not have a free rein. They are acting on behalf of the management committee and should report regularly on what they are doing.

MAKING SURE THINGS GET DONE

If your management committee is made up mainly of people who come to meetings but do little in between you could run into problems getting things done. This problem is likely to be more acute in groups with no paid workers. To make sure decisions made by your management committee are carried out you need to:

● *Decide not just what will be done but who will do it and how* – try to share the load so that too much does not fall to the most willing volunteer, like Sally.

● *Agree a time scale* – what will be done by the next meeting?

● *Make it clear when you will expect a progress report* – for example, at the next meeting.

In groups with paid staff the problems can be somewhat different. In these groups members of the management committee often take it for granted that 'the staff' will do all the work necessary to carry out decisions – even when 'the staff' consists of a single, part-time worker.

Getting the balance right and establishing a good working relationship between paid staff and their management committee is not always easy. Workers sometimes feel that the management committee interferes when they are not needed yet fails to provide the necessary support when they are. See Chapter 9 for more on employing staff.

Example – managing at a distance

Sam is the only paid worker in a group that provides services for visually impaired people. His is a 'hands-off' management committee. Members turn up to meetings but rarely do anything else. 'The Chair never rings and asks how it is going,' Sam says. 'And at meetings whatever comes up they just say 'Look into that, will you, Sam' or 'Sam will take care of that.'

In fact, Sam prefers this type of committee to one that is too involved in the day-to-day running of the group: 'I would hate to have my management committee breathing down my neck,' he says, but admits he would appreciate more guidance when it comes to deciding priorities and the general direction of the group.

KEEPING RECORDS

Minutes

The minutes of management committee meetings provide a permanent record of the policy decisions taken by the group. Yours should be:

- *Clear.* It should be possible to reconstruct from them the essentials of the meeting: what was decided and why, what was reported, what was discussed and what action is to be taken as a result of the meeting.

- *To the point.* They should sum up discussions, not give every detail of who said what.

- *Unambiguous.* Decisions need to be clear and not open to different interpretations. The minutes should be able to act as a future source of reference on what the group decided in the past.

Gathering statistics

You will also need to decide what other records, if any, your group ought to keep to help you monitor your activities. If you offer a service such as advice or counselling, for example, you will probably want to record the number of people enquiring about the service as well as the number actually using it together with basic details of clients such as sex, age range, perhaps ethnic origin. A convenient way to collect such information is to design a simple form to be filled in for each client.

Statistical records like these give you some idea of the level of demand for your service which can help you make a case when applying for funding. They can also help you to build a picture of who is and who is not using your service, giving your management committee a basis for making policy.

Confidentiality

Statistical information can be kept anonymously. If your group keeps more detailed records about individual cases you will need to think hard about confidentiality. Your management committee will need to consider:

● *Why you need to keep this information.* Just because someone consults you about a problem it does not automatically follow that you need to keep details of the problem on your files. Are you keeping more information than you strictly need?

● *Where you should keep the information.* How can you make sure confidential information is maximally secure?

● *Who should see the information.* How will you control who has access to the information you keep?

Computer records

Under the Data Protection Act 1984, if you keep information about clients or any other people on computer you need to register with the Data Protection Registrar. The information you keep does not need to be particularly personal for you to need to register – it could be as little as a name and address. Registration is for three years and forms and information leaflets are available from the Office of the Data Protection Registrar (see the list of addresses at the end of the book).

CHECKLIST

To get things done your group needs an effective management committee. To make your management committee effective, the key areas to think about are:

● *Committee membership* – have you got the right mix of people to suit the needs of your group?

● *Responsibilities* – is everyone clear about the role and responsibilities of the committee?

- *Setting up* – have you followed the procedures for setting up the committee laid down in your constitution?

- *Officers* – what roles do you need the Chair, Secretary and Treasurer to play in your group?

- *Committee training* – would your committee benefit from an initial training session?

- *Committee meetings* – are you clear what has to be done before, during and after your committee meetings?

- *Limits of authority* – is everyone clear who has the authority to do what?

- *Effectiveness* – can you be confident your committee's decisions will actually be carried out?

- *Records* – what records does your group need to keep and why?

TALKING POINTS

- Members of the management committee of a voluntary group take on a heavy responsibility. Do you think this stops more people from becoming involved?

- Are you having problems getting people to serve on your management committee? If so, why do you think this is?

- Management committees can get cut off from the rest of the organisation. How does your management committee keep the rest of the group in touch with what is going on?

3
How to Manage Volunteers

WHY PEOPLE VOLUNTEER

> I couldn't work without my volunteers. They are really great. They see what they do as two-way – they are helping people who need support but they are getting a lot out of it for themselves at the same time.
>
> (Sheila, volunteer co-ordinator in a hospital for the elderly)

Though volunteers work without pay, this does not mean they work for nothing. People who give their time and energy for free do expect to get something back. Some volunteers know exactly what they want, whether it is work experience or just company. Others only realise what they wanted when they don't get it.

People volunteer for all kinds of reasons. Write down as many reasons as you can think of, then compare your list with the one below.

Some reasons for volunteering

● *Gain new skills/work experience* – some people see volunteering as a step on the way to, or back to, paid employment.

● *Give something back to society* – some volunteers are very conscious of being one of the 'haves' and feel a strong need to put something back into their community.

● *Help provide a service they need* – parents will help run a nursery, for example, because they need the child care it offers.

● *Make friends* – volunteers for a common cause can sometimes become very close.

- *Fill time* – for some people time hangs heavily on their hands especially after they retire or if they lose their job. Volunteering can give them back a sense of purpose.

- *Do something completely different* – for many people the work they do as a volunteer is poles apart from their paid job or other every-day activities.

- *Have fun* – some kinds of voluntary work are very challenging and give volunteers a real buzz.

You can probably add lots of other reasons to this list as could your co-organisers who will each have their own reason for getting involved in your group. Discuss with them why they give their time if you don't know already, then talk to some of your volunteers about why they came on board.

Round pegs in round holes

According to the National Association of Volunteer Bureaux, 'a volunteer's expectations of what they will gain from volunteering should shape the nature of the work and duties they undertake as a volunteer.' For many volunteers this simply does not happen. When Edith was widowed a friend who was active in a local charity suggested she might like to help with fund-raising. Edith agreed mainly for the company only to spend her first afternoon as a volunteer addressing envelopes all on her own.

If you want to keep the goodwill of your volunteers you should try to take their needs into account as far as you practically can. It is important to:

- talk to them early on about what they hope to gain from the group;
- be realistic as to whether the group can meet their needs.

Why Carol volunteered to help run her local nursery

'I was working full-time and needed child care. Our local nursery was ideal for me, practically next door. It was run by parents and it was made pretty clear to me I'd have to be on the management committee. We did try and get people on who weren't parents but it didn't really work out. I'd had some experience of doing accounts so I soon found myself elected as treasurer which meant I had to do all the books – there was never enough money to pay someone. In all I was on the committee for nearly six years.'

Why Emma volunteered to help run her local community radio group

'The idea really appealed to me – ordinary people making their own radio programmes about things that really mattered. I'd just left my job which was in marketing and while I was looking around I got very involved with the group helping them get sponsorship and doing a lot of their publicity. It felt much more worthwhile than what I'd been doing before.'

Why Jim volunteered to be an advice worker

'I didn't really want to retire, it was my doctor who advised me to ease up. I'd been running my own business and working all the hours God sent. I finally gave in but I was determined I wasn't going to vegetate. I still felt I had a lot to offer so I applied to be an advice worker at the local Citizens Advice Bureau. The training was quite an eye-opener. At my age I didn't think I had a lot to learn – how wrong can you be!'

Volunteers Charter

Volunteer Bureaux offer an advice and placement service to people who want to become volunteers as well as promoting good practice in volunteering. The National Association of Volunteer Bureaux have produced a Charter (see p. 54) to help volunteers get a fair deal.

WHAT'S SPECIAL ABOUT MANAGING VOLUNTEERS?

Some people argue that there is nothing special about volunteer staff. Anyone who works as a volunteer should be entitled, except for pay, to all the same terms and conditions of service as paid workers in the organisation. Some groups are taking positive steps to put this ideal into practice.

This view may well make sense in larger organisations where volunteers work alongside sizeable numbers of paid workers. Under pressure to act more like businesses, some charities and voluntary groups are trying hard to improve the way they manage their staff including their volunteers.

For volunteers like Ian this can only be for the good: 'The worst thing I have found about being a volunteer is the lack of status. You get all the rotten jobs to do. The best organisations I know are the ones that look after their volunteers – make it possible for them to get together and have some say in the way the group is run.'

VOLUNTEERS CHARTER

1. Volunteers should have a clear idea of the tasks they are being asked to perform and of the responsibility that goes with these tasks.

2. Volunteers should know who is designated as having responsibility for their support and supervision. Volunteers should have regular access to this person, and the person should ensure that each volunteer is adequately supported.

3. To ensure fair representation of the needs and interests of volunteers, volunteers should have access to, and play a part in, the decision making process of the group/organisation for whom they are working as volunteers.

4. Volunteers should be protected against exploitation of their interests, both as individuals and as volunteers. Volunteers should not be put under any moral pressure to do work which goes against their principles.

5. Volunteers should be adequately protected against any risks which may arise from doing voluntary work. Volunteers should, for instance, be covered by Public Liability Insurance.

6. Volunteers should not suffer financial loss through doing voluntary work. Volunteers should receive out of pocket expenses and be provided with appropriate equipment/ tools/materials to enable them to carry out their tasks.

7. Volunteers should not be used in place of previously paid workers.

8. The relationship between paid workers and volunteers should be complementary and mutually beneficial. Paid workers in an organisation should be fully aware of the areas of work undertaken by volunteers and of the responsibilities of both themselves and volunteers.

9. Volunteers should have the right to join a trade union relevant to the work in which they are involved. The organisation using volunteers' help should encourage volunteers to take up union membership. The Manufacturing Science and Finance (MSF) Union and NUPE now offer free membership to volunteers and specifically target volunteers' needs and interests.

10. Volunteering should be a fulfilling experience. Through adequate support and supervision, volunteers should be able to develop, expand and change their area of work.

Vive la difference!

Many volunteers, of course, do not see themselves in the same light as paid workers. Some positively value the difference, particularly the freedom they feel as volunteers. Pat had decided to take a break from paid employment and volunteered to help with the administration of a local welfare rights group. She is highly committed, very efficient and always makes sure things get done even when domestic commitments occasionally mean she cannot do her stint. For her: 'It's great not to feel guilty when I can't come into the office.' This absence of guilt she puts down to being a volunteer.

Voting with their feet

Pat feels differently because there is a difference between being a volunteer and being a paid worker. Though some groups are trying to blur the distinction the fact remains that:

- volunteers can vote with their feet.

If they do not like the way the group is run or the way they are treated or what they are asked to do, they can simply walk away. Just like that. And sometimes they do.

   Some groups, particularly major national organisations such as the Citizens Advice Bureaux Service, ask volunteers to commit themselves for a certain length of time after training. And in practice, of course, many volunteers are, if anything, more committed than paid staff. But some are more like Steve who joined his local hospital radio, full of enthusiasm, keen to do anything and everything. A month later he got a job as a trainee reporter on the local paper – and was never seen again.

Example – getting a better offer

Your group has no hold over your volunteers, as Andrea found when she arranged a meeting with a senior manager at the local hospital and the sister in charge of the main children's ward. Andrea chairs a group concerned with the needs of sick children and she was going to the meeting with one of their volunteers until: 'Right at the last minute I get this call with some feeble excuse why she couldn't come. It was too late for me to get hold of anyone else. Some volunteers are like that – they get a better offer, something comes up they would rather do. Luckily the majority are much more committed.'

Making people feel valued

Though you cannot prevent volunteers from having their own agenda you can try hard to create the kind of organisation in which people feel valued and appreciated and don't want to let the others down. You need to aim for:

- *An open, welcoming atmosphere* – some groups feel cliquish or dominated by overbearing personalities.

- *Clear responsibilities* – people need to know what is expected of them and who they can turn to if things go wrong.

- *Plenty of support* – so that no one carries too much of a load and everyone feels loyal to the group.

Try and imagine how your group appears to outsiders. If you are not sure, talk to one of your recent recruits. Find out how they felt coming along for the first time.

RECRUITING VOLUNTEERS

Some people are wary of voluntary organisations usually because they have had their fingers burnt. 'They can really mess you around,' says Ted who volunteered to help out at a local Day Centre. He went for an interview then heard absolutely nothing. Maybe the organisers felt Ted was unsuitable but, if so, they should at least have had the decency to tell him. Ted's self-confidence was already fragile before the interview, now it is non-existent.

Before bringing in other people you and your co-organisers need to agree:

- *What you want volunteers to do* – don't expect them to invent their own jobs or see what is required without being told.

- *How many volunteers you need* – if you recruit too many and don't give them enough to do they will soon lose interest.

- *How you will decide if a particular volunteer is suitable* – what qualities are you looking for? Which are the most important?

- *How you will handle volunteers who are not suitable* – can you use them in other ways? If not, when and how will you let them know?

ALLREAD PROJECT

JOB DESCRIPTION

Job Title: Volunteer Reader
Responsible to: Project Co-ordinator
Time commitment: Normally 2-3 hours a week
Place of work: Various locations in Allbury

Aims of the project

To provide a reading service for visually impaired people. Volunteers normally visit clients in their homes to read them letters, newspaper/magazine articles or anything else they need. Volunteers sometimes also help with writing tasks such as form filling.

Tasks

- Visiting visually impaired people in their homes when asked by the Project Co-ordinator

- Reading aloud letters, articles or any other material, as required

- Occasionally helping with writing tasks such as form filling

- Attending monthly volunteer meetings

- Attending any training felt to be required

Skills and experience needed

Sympathetic manner. Patience and sensitivity to people's needs. Ability to read aloud and clearly and to carry out basic writing tasks such as filling in forms.

Fig. 5. Job description for a volunteer.

Job descriptions

To help you recruit volunteers successfully you will find it useful to borrow from the world of paid work the idea of drawing up:

- job descriptions for the various types of work you want volunteers to do;
- descriptions of the skills and experience you are looking for (known in personnel jargon as 'person specifications').

A job description is what it says it is – a written description of the various tasks that make up the job the volunteer will do (see fig. 5). You would normally include:

- Job title.
- Place of work.

- Time commitment required.
- What the volunteer will be expected to do (including any meetings or other events they are required to attend).

Putting together a job description is a very useful exercise because it forces you to spell out the tasks you want volunteers to do rather than leaving them vague. Try putting together a job description for your own job in the group. Suggest to your co-organisers they do the same for their jobs then get together and compare the results. This is a very good way of bringing out into the open any confusion over who does what.

Getting the right person

Some jobs can be done by almost anyone. Visiting long-stay patients in hospital, for example. A poster asking for volunteers gave a very simple 'person specification':

'No qualifications necessary, just a little free time and a caring attitude'

For other jobs you may feel you need people with more specific qualifications such as word processing or DIY skills or experience of running theatre workshops or coaching football.

Example – horses for courses

Groups often need various kinds of volunteers for different types of work. Neville is the co-ordinator of a reading service for visually impaired people. To run the service he needs volunteers to do two kinds of job: (1) to read books on to tape and (2) to visit visually impaired people in their homes to read letters or short articles to them and possibly help them write letters or fill in forms.

The qualities required for these two types of job are very different. For reading books on to tape, Neville looks for people with the right kind of voice. Before taking anyone on he gets them to do a voice test. 'I get them to read a sample from a book which we send out to users of the service for them to tell us whether they think the voice makes for pleasant and easy listening.' If it doesn't Neville has to turn the volunteer down.

For the other job, visiting people in their homes, Neville is more concerned with personal qualities such as patience and sensitivity. 'Of course they do have to read, but for this job it is their personality not their voice that decides whether they are suitable.'

Don't rule people out too quickly

When thinking about the kinds of volunteers you need for your group:

- *Don't exclude anyone unnecessarily.* Only ask for specific qualifications if they are really essential. If Neville had insisted on a voice test for volunteers visiting people in their homes to read them letters, for example, this could have unnecessarily ruled out many suitable people.

- *Try to see beyond people like yourselves.* Some groups don't so much turn away people who seem to be different as make them feel they are not going to fit.

- *Try to use people who offer help if you possibly can.* You may need to use your imagination to come up with something they can usefully do. One group, for example, needed volunteers to staff their telephone helpline. The phone was in their office up two narrow flights of stairs in a building without a lift. This appeared to rule out Veronica who is confined to a wheelchair but rather than lose her the co-ordinator asked her to take on another, rather different role. Veronica writes letters to papers and magazines about anything and everything relating to the group. 'If we see something in the *Sun* or wherever that really annoys us we ring Veronica and she gets hold of the paper and writes the letter and sends us a copy. If it was left to us we'd never have the time.'

Application forms

If you regularly recruit volunteers you will probably want to design an application form. Some people find forms offputting so you will need to keep yours simple and ask only for information you absolutely need. Look at the forms other groups use to give you ideas. Most application forms ask for:

- Name, address and phone number
- Details of any work experience, voluntary or paid
- Qualifications/training courses attended/special skills
- Interests/any community work done
- How much time available
- Names of two referees

You will also need to consider whether to include a section on the form asking volunteers to give details of any relevant criminal record. This is particularly important if they will be visiting clients in their homes or working with people who may be vulnerable. Make it clear that having a criminal record does not automatically mean they will be turned down – you will need to look at each case on its merits.

Rehabilitation of Offenders Act 1974
This Act allows offences to be considered 'spent' after a certain period of time so offenders no longer need to declare them. There are exceptions, however, and these include people who will be working with vulnerable groups such as children or the mentally ill. These people must disclose all previous convictions. If your volunteers will be working with any vulnerable groups you will need to make it clear on your form that all offences must be disclosed however long ago they were committed.

WHERE TO FIND VOLUNTEERS

One of the simplest ways to get people to volunteer is to ask them. In a major survey of volunteering commissioned by the Volunteer Centre UK, half those questioned said they got involved in volunteering because they were asked. Word of mouth is a very effective means of recruiting new volunteers particularly if you only need small numbers. The downside is that you could easily end up with a group of people too much the same.

Other ways you can attract volunteers include:

- *Local media.* Send a press release to your local paper and local radio station telling them about your group and explaining what you need volunteers to do.

- *Giving talks about your group.* This is a good way of gaining publicity for the group's activities as well as attracting new volunteers.

- *Posters, leaflets.* Design a simple poster and/or information leaflet for display in community centres, libraries, church halls, etc. (see fig. 6).

- *Volunteer Bureaux.* These act as a kind of agency matching people wanting to do voluntary work with organisations that need them. You can give them details of your volunteer vacancies. There are around 300 Bureaux in the UK. Look under V in the telephone book.

- *REACH.* The Retired Executives Action Clearing-House is a very useful organisation which places retired (or redundant) people with professional or business skills on an expenses-only basis in voluntary groups that need their expertise.

- *The Volunteer Centre UK database.* The Volunteer Centre UK has a national database of volunteering opportunities called Signposts. They will send you a form where you can list your group's activities and the kinds of tasks you need volunteers to do. These details will be sent to anyone in your area who wants to volunteer. They also run a UK Volunteers Week every year which normally produces thousands of enquiries from people wanting to do voluntary work.

It takes all sorts . . .

Jack's group works on their local moor trying to improve the wildlife habitat, suppress bracken and regenerate the heather:

> In a novel attempt to recruit extra hands Jack took to photographing and apprehending poachers, whom he would give the option of putting in a few hours on the moor or of being reported to the authorities. Unfortunately, as he remarked, 'the majority of those caught seem to have a greater fear of work that they do of the police.'
>
> *(The Independent)*

Fig. 6. Poster to attract volunteers.

INTERVIEWING NEW RECRUITS

If your group is desperate for helpers you may be tempted just to grab any volunteer that comes along. Don't. Talk to them before you take them on. Ask them to come in for a 'chat' if you think the word 'interview' seems too formal. Make it clear the chat or interview is two-way – volunteers need to judge whether your group suits them as much as you need to judge whether they are right for you.

Though it is important to interview volunteers, it is not actually that easy to interview well. Judy went for an interview with the organisers of a group that helps people with eating disorders: 'I thought I was being interviewed to be a counsellor but it turned out they really needed a co-ordinator. It was all very confusing.'

Most people have had experience of bad interviews. Think about your own experience. What was the worst? Note down what was particularly bad about it. Which was the best interview you ever had? Note down what made it so good.

To interview well you need to be clear what you are looking for and what you want the interview to achieve. Generally when interviewing volunteers you will be looking for the answers to two basic questions:

- *Does this person have the right qualities for the job?* You are not obliged to take someone just because they offer. If you need someone with commitment and energy, for example, where is the evidence that commitment and energy is what they have?

- *Can the group offer this person what they want?* If they are looking for an outlet for their creativity and you want them to organise your press cuttings file, will that be sufficiently creative or will they soon get bored?

Example – in-depth interviewing

Paul is one of the organisers of a group whose volunteers offer homeless young people a bed for the night while they are helped to find more permanent accommodation. He interviews potential recruits in their own homes which gives him the opportunity to see the room the young person would be staying in. 'The interview can take a long time – at least $1^1/2$ hours and often as long as $2^1/2$ hours. I talk about practical sides of the scheme like insurance and expenses and the police check we have to do on all our volunteers. Then I ask three questions. The first is about their own experience of family life and leaving home – some people talk and talk about what happened to them and often the reason why they want to volunteer with us comes out at this stage. I then ask them about their own experience of homelessness – some only know about it through the media, others have been homeless themselves at some time in their life. The third question is about their hopes and fears in volunteering with us. What I'm looking for all the time are signs of their attitudes – we don't want people who are harsh or critical or judgmental.'

Tips for interviewing volunteers

- *Introduce yourself* – and anyone else present. Paul's type of in-depth interview is probably best done on his own. You might find it easier to interview with one of your co-organisers. Take a little time over the introductions making clear your positions in the group – too many people emerge from interviews with a very hazy idea of who they have seen.

- *Ask open questions* – the kind that start with question words such as what, how, where. Get the volunteer to talk about their interests including any previous voluntary work. Try and find out what they think they are good at and what they feel they have to offer.

- *Find out what the volunteer hopes to gain from their work with the group* – be honest about whether they are likely to get it.

- *Be clear about the kind of commitment you expect* – find out what else they are doing. Some people volunteer for several groups and then find difficulty in meeting all their obligations.

- *Tell them what will happen next* – when will they hear, will you be taking up references, when would they start. If they really are unsuitable, remember – it's tough being turned down for voluntary work. Think about tactful ways of saying no.

Volunteers on welfare benefits

If you take on volunteers on welfare benefits (apart from pensions) encourage them to tell their benefits office they are volunteering. For sick and disabled people the rules have been eased so they can now do

16 hours a week of voluntary work without their benefit being affected. Volunteers on unemployment benefit must remain available for full-time work and be actively seeking work. For details see the Benefits Agency booklet: *Voluntary and Part-Time Workers* (FB26).

TAKING UP REFERENCES

As well as interviewing new recruits you should also take up references particularly if volunteers will be visiting people in their homes. If your volunteers will be working with children a police check may also be necessary.

Example – what can happen when you are desperate

Groups that don't take up references have sometimes got their fingers burnt. One group was desperate for an office administrator. They had no paid workers and mail could sometimes pile up for days. Nick was a very plausible young man who turned up out of the blue and offered to help. He had the run of the office and no one noticed the letters he was sending out on the group's headed paper asking for money for crazy projects he dreamt up himself. The Chair only found out when one of the agencies Nick had contacted rang her and asked for an explanation. Though she tried to limit the damage the group still ended up looking foolish while Nick for his part could not see what all the fuss was about. He thought he was doing an excellent job and only stepped down under protest. The whole episode left a very sour taste – and the group still doesn't have an administrator.

Tips for taking up references

● *Send the referee a copy of the job description.* They need to know what kind of work the volunteer will be doing to be able to say whether they are suitable.

● *Take up references before the volunteer starts work.* Don't wait till things start going wrong. Brenda who runs a Day Centre learnt this lesson the hard way. 'I had this volunteer, a woman who seemed too good to be true. She was very good with the old people but then I started to get the feeling she was taking over the place. She wanted to come in every day and I could see she upset some of the other staff. I realised I should have asked her for references so I took her aside one day and said I needed two names. She got really emotional and kept insisting she was good at the job but in the end she did give me a couple of names. They turned out to be people she'd worked for so long ago they didn't remember her. When I took this up with her she stormed out and never came back.'

● *Use the information about strengths and weaknesses.* Try and match the volunteer with the tasks that suit them best.

● *Try and keep an open mind.* If there is something in a reference you are not happy about try, if it seems reasonable, to give the volunteer a chance to give their side of the story.

● *Keep references confidential.* Don't leave written references lying around the office where anyone could see them.

HELPING VOLUNTEERS SETTLE IN

First impressions count in voluntary groups like everywhere else. New recruits can be nervous about coming along for the first time especially if they don't know anyone in the group. If no one makes them feel welcome they may just turn on their heels and leave.

Induction

Someone needs to take new volunteers under their wing when they first come along. It needs to be someone's specific responsibility to introduce them to the others, explain how things work and tell them what they are supposed to do. You might also find it useful to put together an information sheet for volunteers laying out what they need to know. For example:

● who's who in the organisation
● some do's and don'ts
● basic procedures
● essential phone numbers
● who to ask if they need help

Think about it – if you were a volunteer joining your group what would you need to know? Make a list then discuss with your co-organisers whether this should go into an information sheet or pack for your volunteers.

TRAINING VOLUNTEERS

Volunteers need to be trained for some kinds of jobs especially those concerned with advice work and counselling. Most volunteers see training in a positive light though some can be worried by the idea, afraid they may look stupid or be unable to make the grade. These are often people who end up doing very well but in the early stages they may need a bit of extra reassurance.

If you are planning to set up a training programme for volunteers you will need to consider:

- *What kind of training?* How much experience of training do you and your co-organisers have between you? Have you talked to similar groups elsewhere? What kind of training do they offer?

- *Who will do the training?* Can a more established group help? For example, volunteers working for the AIDS helpline discussed earlier got some initial training from the Terrence Higgins Trust in both how to run a phoneline and how to organise their group.

- *Will the training be part of your selection process?* If volunteers will have to complete the training course successfully before being finally accepted, you will need to make this clear at the interview stage.

- *When will the training be held?* Evenings? Weekends? During the day? Will the time of day rule out any particular group? How often will you run courses?

- *How much will it cost?* Will you have to pay an outside trainer? Book a hall?

Example – cut out for the job?

One of the advantages of training is that volunteers can start to see for themselves whether they are really cut out for doing the job. Jan runs the volunteer training for a telephone helpline for victims of rape: 'Our training can be quite intense and some people can't take it. Usually we don't even have to say anything – they realise for themselves that this kind of work isn't right for them.'

Improving skills

As your volunteers gain experience they will want to improve their skills. One way is to run occasional day or half-day training sessions around issues arising from the work of the group. Can you think of any suitable topics your group might tackle on such training days? Are there particular problems or issues volunteers have been facing? Discuss with your co-organisers how you might put a training day together.

GIVING FEEDBACK AND SUPPORT

Some kinds of voluntary work can be very challenging, sometimes draining, occasionally harrowing. Volunteers working in winter night shelters for homeless people, for instance, can sometimes have to deal with drugs or alcohol problems or violence flaring up. Some burn out before the winter is over.

Most volunteering is not quite that dramatic but volunteers still often need someone to turn to for advice and support. Groups have numerous ways of supporting their volunteer workers:

- *A volunteer co-ordinator or volunteer organiser* – someone whose job it is to see to the needs of volunteers. This really should be a paid post but if you have no money to pay staff then possibly a small team of two or three can share the responsibility.

- *Regular support meetings* – where volunteers can get together to discuss cases or problems and explore experiences and ideas.

- *Creating a supportive atmosphere* – where volunteers feel they can contact each other whenever they need to talk something over. To make this easy you can give everyone a contacts list with the addresses and phone numbers of the other volunteers.

- *Regular reviews* – sessions where volunteers have an opportunity to look back over their work with the group, pick out what went well and what went less well, air any problems or grievances. If you do not have a volunteer co-ordinator then a small team of you can carry out these reviews. Don't forget to review one another too.

- *Networks* – new groups are sometimes taken under the wing of more established groups and learn from them. Sometimes co-ordinators of different groups get together to exchange ideas. Citizens Advice Bureau workers are starting to set up regional networks organised by volunteers for volunteers – the aim is to provide both support and a platform for volunteers to air their views and get them heard.

Keeping an eye on things

Problems are more likely to arise if volunteers are just left to their own devices. However busy you and your co-organisers are, somebody needs to be around to keep an eye on new recruits. This is particularly important if part of their job is to answer the phone.

To anyone phoning in for the first time the person who answers *is* your organisation. 'We sometimes have to be very diplomatic and tactful with people who ring in,' says Bob who runs the group that takes in unwanted furniture for distribution to people who need it. 'People assume we will take anything they want to get rid of but in fact the furniture needs to be in reasonable condition. If it is a bed we need to find out about the state of the mattress, whether it is stained. There are ways and ways of asking questions like that.'

There are also ways and ways of helping volunteers improve their telephone technique. People are sometimes brusque because they are nervous or not confident about what to say. Criticising them directly will probably make them even less confident. Try taking them aside and asking them how they felt the call went. Talk to them about it – try to get them to see for themselves what went wrong. Giving constructive criticism isn't easy. 'Some volunteers act as though they are doing you a favour,' says one co-ordinator. 'It can be very difficult to get them to improve their standards when they think you should be grateful they are doing anything at all.'

Picking up problems

If people don't complain it is tempting to assume they do not have any problems. In fact they may simply be complaining behind your back. You need to make a positive effort to ask people how they are getting on – if they think you really want to know they will probably tell you rather than moan to each other.

Example – when problems are not obvious

Some problems just aren't obvious unless you ask. Janet joined her local victim support group but did not really settle down. When she was asked to visit a client she often said it was too short notice. If she wasn't asked to visit she complained there wasn't enough work. Eventually it came out that Janet liked to plan ahead – she had really been looking for voluntary work she could do regularly once a week on a certain day rather than whenever a case came up. Just airing her feelings seemed to make Janet feel better while the co-ordinator of the group tried to give her more notice of when she would be needed.

DEVELOPING AN EQUAL OPPORTUNITIES POLICY

When you start a voluntary group you have the opportunity to build in a positive approach to equality of opportunity. You and your co-organisers can make it clear right from the start that volunteers will be offered work purely on the basis of their suitability for the task. No volunteer, no member of the group, no user of your services will be discriminated against because of their gender, age, marital status, responsibilities for dependants, race or ethnic origin, religion, sexual orientation or disabilities. Many groups have a written equal opportunities policy to this effect.

After you have been up and running for a time you may want to take a look at how far your convictions have turned themselves into action. Look at:

- *The make-up of your management committee.* How representative is it of the local population in terms of age, gender, ethnic groups? Why do you think some groups are under-represented? What do you think may be the effect?

- *Users of your services.* Have you been monitoring the take-up of your services by different groups? Are there any groups who rarely use your service? Do you know why?

- *Your procedures for recruiting volunteers.* Are you excluding any groups without realising it? Could you publicise yourselves more widely? Should you be targeting particular groups?

CHECKLIST

When managing volunteers the key areas to think about are:

- *Why people volunteer* – what do your volunteers hope to gain from working with the group?

- *What's different about volunteers* – so you can plan realistically.
- *Recruitment* – what do you want people to do and what kinds of people do you need?
- *Interviews* – how can you best find out what you need to know?
- *References* – why these are important.
- *Induction* – how to get your volunteers off to a good start.
- *Training* – does your group need a training programme?
- *Feedback and support* – how can you best support your volunteers?
- *Equal opportunities* – how good is your group's record?

TALKING POINTS

- What do you see as the main differences (apart from pay) between volunteers and paid workers?

- What do you think of the Volunteers Charter?

- What kind of image does the term 'volunteer' conjure up – is it positive or negative?

- How easily could a volunteer confined to a wheelchair work with your group?

4
Operating Day-to-Day

DO YOU NEED A CO-ORDINATOR?

Different groups have very different workloads as we saw in Chapter 1.
Remember Dennis, the retired builder who set up a local history group?
For him the group was an engrossing hobby. He loved all the business
of organising speakers and dealing with membership and doing the
books. He had a small committee but they didn't meet very often because Dennis liked to do everything himself. The others used to mutter
about this – but that's another story.

The AIDS helpline was very different. Where Dennis's workload
stayed constant with his group holding the same kinds of meetings with
the same kinds of speakers year after year, the helpline really took off.
Work expanded but though the group had premises and enough funds to
run the phoneline and train their volunteers they could not afford any
paid staff. Nikki took on the role of unpaid co-ordinator which turned out
to be very much a full-time job. 'If I took time off I'd come back in and
find four days' mail piled up. The job completely took over my life.'

Key figures
Dennis and Nikki are at two extremes with Dennis giving a few hours a
week to running a group that interests him and Nikki giving up a huge
chunk of her life to a group for which she felt deep commitment. Yet
they have something in common in spite of their groups being so different – they are both key figures.

Voluntary groups often have a key figure that everyone identifies
with, the person who holds all the threads together, knows what is going
on and represents the group to the outside world. This key figure could
be the co-ordinator/administrator or the Chair of the management committee or simply the person who first set the group up.

Groups need these key figures especially in their early stages –
people with commitment and vision who can inspire others and get

them to give of their best. But key figures can also cause problems. They can be like Dennis and insist on keeping everything in their own hands. Or they may go on too long and inspire irritation instead of affection.

Or, more difficult, they might be too dedicated and go far beyond the call of duty. Volunteers are not protected by employment laws, they do not necessarily have fixed hours or overtime. If they are really committed and playing a key role, they may just go on and on and on. Others do not always notice quite how much weight they are carrying until they fall ill or burn out or move on leaving a gaping hole.

Danger signs

The moral of all this is that groups should not rely too heavily on one person particularly if that person is a volunteer. Think about your own group. Is there a key figure that everyone turns to? What would happen to the group were that person suddenly to disappear?

These are some of the danger signs to look out for:

- One central person holds most of the important information.
- Things get left undone when this person is away – no one steps in.
- This central person takes on more and more and doesn't ask for help.

Taking on a paid co-ordinator

We started this chapter with a question: Do you need a co-ordinator? The least misleading answer is: it depends. If your workload is expanding and you can raise the money to take on a paid-co-ordinator to hold the group together then, yes, it is probably a good idea.

But if you do take this route you need to take care not to overload your one paid worker particularly if they are only part-time. Sometimes groups that have been struggling finally find the funds to employ a worker, breathe a collective sigh of relief and withdraw much of their labour leaving their unfortunate employee to flounder around on their own. (See Chapter 9 for more on employing staff.)

Relying on a voluntary co-ordinator

If you cannot afford to pay a co-ordinator you may be able to find someone willing to do the job voluntarily. But you need to be aware of the very real danger that, like Nikki in the early days, the group will take over this volunteer's life. If someone is willing to take on the role of unpaid co-ordinator you need to make sure they have plenty of support. Some people simply take on too much and need saving from themselves.

Setting up teams

Instead of a single co-ordinator you can spread the load by having two or three central figures who communicate regularly. You can also set up teams to take responsibility for areas such as administration, training, publicity – these may be the same as or offshoots of the sub-committees of your management committee discussed in Chapter 2.

Whatever you decide, it is extremely important to:

- *Be realistic.* If your resources are limited, do as much as you can and don't feel guilty about not doing more. Local authorities and other funding bodies can expect an awful lot from voluntary groups that offer services within their community. If you feel under pressure from funders to achieve more, use this as an argument for getting money for paid staff.

WHAT NEEDS TO BE DONE?

Some groups find it easier than others to keep their workload under control. Some self-help groups, for example, are in a position to do as much or as little as they like depending on the enthusiasm of their members. Environmental groups may well have an ambitious programme but if their membership drops off they can always decide to do less.

The kinds of groups that can find themselves under pressure are those that offer services within their community. If their volunteers dwindle in number organisers can come under a lot of strain as they try to carry on so as not to let users down.

Example – carrying on regardless

A local branch of the Multiple Sclerosis Society run entirely by volunteers found themselves getting very stretched as more and more MS sufferers contacted them for help. In this group volunteers work mainly as ambulance drivers and as welfare visitors making sure people with MS know how to get the practical help they need and lending a sympathetic ear to their worries. The organisers put an SOS in their local paper and that produced a few possible volunteers. 'It's very difficult to recruit new volunteers,' says one of the organisers. 'We could do with twice as many. So often the people with MS contacting us now are young with small children. Some are facing tremendous difficulties. We cope because we have some wonderful old stalwarts who are always willing to take on new cases. Without them, I don't know what we would do.'

What are the tasks?
When time is short and organisers are stretched the jobs most often done in haste or not done at all are those to do with the administration of the group. Grant applications are sometimes cobbled together at the last minute. Opportunities for publicity go by the board as no one has time to plan ahead.

A useful exercise
You will stand a better chance of getting the essential tasks done if everyone can agree what these are. Try this exercise with your co-organisers. You will need a flipchart or large sheet of paper:

● Start by listing all the tasks that need doing to keep your group running smoothly. Include day-to-day tasks such as dealing with correspondence and buying stamps, occasional tasks such as inter-viewing new volunteers and once a year tasks such as organising the AGM or making grant applications. The order you put them in doesn't matter.

● Now think about the categories each of these tasks fall into such as administration, publicity, finance, recruitment, etc. Decide which of the categories each task belongs in. Mark each task on the list with the initial of the category (A for admin, P for publicity and so on). You should now begin to see if you have a lot more tasks in one category than another – is this to be expected or is something going wrong?

● Next mark each task with the initials of the person or people responsible for it at the moment.

● Finally, look at your results critically. Does the distribution make sense? Does the same person do a number of tasks in the same category or is everyone all over the place? Is someone doing far too much? Are people happy with what they are doing? Do some people want a change? Are some important tasks no one's respon-sibility?

Example – three kinds of work

Exercises like this are useful because they help turn a general mass of work into identifiable tasks. Nikki, the voluntary co-ordinator of the AIDS helpline, eventually became the paid co-ordinator – and continued to do all the hours under the sun. As the group developed and funding increased it became possible to employ more staff. To find out what the group most needed Nikki wrote down everything she did and how long it took over a six-month period. From this it became clear that there were three main strands to the work she had been doing: co-ordinating volunteers, administration and development/project work. The group now has three part-time staff responsible for these three different areas.

Tips for getting things done

- *Work out ways of using help efficiently.* It is easier to get more people involved in running the group if you can break down work into individual tasks that can then be handed out. People who do a lot often fall into the trap of feeling that it is usually quicker and easier to do things themselves. Though you may have to explain a job the first or even the second time round, it can be worth the time if someone then takes it on regularly.

- *Use all the help available.* Get support and advice from field workers or other regional staff if you are part of a national organisation; if your local Council has support workers for voluntary groups, use them; talk to your local Council for Voluntary Service or Rural Community Council – don't waste time reinventing anything from scratch.

- *Keep looking forward.* Many groups struggle to keep on top of day-to-day demands leaving no energy or enthusiasm for developing the group. But this is short-sighted. Looking for opportunities to make new contacts and take on new challenges can help keep up enthusiasm and bring in new blood.

GETTING HOLD OF EQUIPMENT

Your office may be only a cubby hole but to your group it is home – and like all homes it needs furnishing even if it's just a desk, a chair or two and a filing cabinet. The trick is to avoid spending money if you possibly can:

- *Talk to the previous tenant* – are they prepared to leave anything behind?

- *Ask around* – is anyone moving house? Or buying new furniture and wanting to get rid of the old? Is a local firm moving to new premises – could they be casting off old office equipment?

- *Look for sponsorship for specific items* – if you can't beg or borrow you can sometimes persuade someone else to pay. One group got the cash for their phone and answer machine from their local radio station that raises money for charity annually in a listeners' Christmas auction.

Example – simplicity itself

A very simple piece of equipment can sometimes make the world of difference. When Pat first got involved in the administration of her local welfare rights group, letters and other papers would come in and lie around for nobody was sure how long. Then Pat had the bright idea of buying a date stamp for the office. From then on every document was date-stamped immediately and passed straight on to the relevant person to deal with. For a small outlay of £3.99 for the stamp and ink pad Pat started a big revolution in running the office.

Knowing what you want

If your group needs other kinds of equipment the same advice applies – beg or borrow rather than buy. Once you know what you want, let it be known. Ask people who may be able to help. Volunteers from a wildlife group were spending evenings from dusk to midnight helping toads cross the road during the spring migration. They talked to local police who were very happy to lend them (the volunteers not the toads) reflective jackets to make their work safer.

A word about computers

Many groups use computers these days mainly for word processing, sometimes for accounts or running a database or desk top publishing. Computers can be invaluable, but they can also be more trouble than they are worth. You need to be particularly wary of:

- *Hand-me-down computers.* You can certainly pick up bargains when a local council or college or company updates their computing system, getting rid of their old machines. However, a second-hand computer, even if it costs next to nothing, is only really a bargain if someone knows how to use it. Hand-me-downs often come without manuals. They may come with or without software. If they do come with software once again you probably won't get the manuals which means someone needs to be already familiar with the word processing or other program. If someone offers you a computer they have no further use for, don't automatically say yes. Only accept it if you know you can use it – don't be lumbered with a white elephant gathering dust and taking up valuable space.

● *Relying too heavily on one computer expert.* Many people still know surprisingly little about computers. Those who do know more than the minimum soon get hailed as experts. If your group relies on a single computer expert consider how you would cope if this person suddenly disappeared. Try and get them to share their expertise by training others to be experts too.

Photocopying

Unless you are a large well-funded group you probably won't have your own photocopier – but you will certainly need access to one. Commercial photocopying is expensive so you need to find a source of cheap copies. Can your local Council for Voluntary Service help? Could you approach a group that does have a machine and make a deal? Or get free or very cheap copies from a local printer as a form of sponsorship, perhaps in exchange for advertising in your publicity leaflets?

HEALTH AND SAFETY

Groups employing volunteers are responsible for ensuring their health and safety at work just as they would be for paid workers. The Health and Safety at Work Act lays down standards which apply to everyone who employs or is employed in either paid or unpaid work.

Thinking about health and safety can suddenly produce feelings of panic as you realise the number of things that could just possibly go wrong. In fact most health and safety requirements are largely common sense. Essentially you need to:

● *Anticipate dangers.* If you have a worn mat or trailing wires, don't just say 'Somebody's going to fall over that one day' – take action before they do.

- *Train people to use equipment properly.* Provide any safety equipment necessary. If certain equipment may only be used by specified people, make this very clear.

- *Don't expect volunteers to work in conditions paid workers would refuse.* Make sure your premises are cleaned regularly, well-lit and kept at a reasonable temperature.

Health and safety checklist

These are the main areas you need to think about. For more detailed advice, talk to your local Health and Safety Executive. Bradford Council for Voluntary Service is also a useful contact point for information on health and safety in the voluntary sector (see list of addresses at the end of the book).

- *Assessing risk.* New regulations on the management of health and safety require you to assess the risks people in your organisation are exposed to when working and show what measures you are taking to minimise those risks.

- *Health and safety policy.* You should have a written policy laying out your group's arrangements for health and safety. The Volunteer Centre UK booklet *Volunteers First* includes a number of sample documents including a health and safety policy. Your local Health and Safety Executive will also give you guidance.

- *First aid.* Your group should have, or have easy access to, a first aid box. Someone in your group needs to be trained in first aid and handling emergencies.

- *Fire.* Do all volunteers know where the exits are? What to do in case of fire? Where the fire extinguishers are and how to use them? Are all fire doors kept shut?

- *Accidents.* You need an accident book and a proper procedure for reporting accidents.

- *Equipment.* Is all your equipment serviced regularly? Are volunteers properly trained? Are you providing any necessary safety equipment?

A test question

To concentrate the mind on safety matters, try this test with one of your co-organisers. Ask them this question: 'You go out to the kitchen to make a cup of coffee, you come back and the waste paper bin is on fire. What would you do?'

ORGANISING PAPERWORK

'Wasn't there a letter from ...?' 'Where do we keep ...?'

Little and often is the secret of keeping on top of paperwork. Mail and messages soon pile up as Nikki found in the days when she was an unpaid co-ordinator. If your group is already struggling to keep its head above water you might find it difficult to arrange cover when key people are away. But you should try at least to have someone come in to open mail and check messages. Leaving letters unanswered and calls unreturned can soon give the impression your group doesn't know what it is doing.

To keep paperwork under control you need to:

- *Get a set of trays and label them* – with the names of people with particular responsibilities. As mail is opened it can go straight into the relevant tray. Someone also needs to make sure these trays are emptied – if people don't come in regularly their mail should be sent on.

- *Set up an office filing system and use it* – if filing isn't done because no one is quite sure where anything belongs, your system isn't working and needs to be rethought.

- *Keep copies of letters sent out* – in some groups all kinds of people send letters on headed paper and you need some way of keeping track. Insist there should be an office copy of every letter.

SETTING UP LINES OF COMMUNICATION

'No one ever seems to know what's going on around here' – or at least that's the way it feels in some groups especially to volunteers nearer the fringes. You will never keep everyone happy but you will keep them happier if you make a positive effort to keep them in touch.

You need to set up clear lines of communication in three areas:

- *In the office* – between the different people involved in the administration of the group.

- *Within the group* – both within the management committee and with the wider membership.

- *With the outside world* – this could include users of your service, funders, local media or anyone else with an interest in what you do.

In the office

If a number of people are involved in the administration of your group they need to keep in touch with what each other is doing. A simple but effective mechanism is to set up a Day Book in which whoever comes into the office notes down anything others need to know and leaves messages about ongoing work that the next person in can pick up (see fig. 7).

Your administrators also need to:

- *Get together regularly* – to review how the office is working and correct any problems.

- *Put procedures in writing* – so new people can take over easily. Volunteers drop out and have to be replaced by people who need to be able to pick up the threads. They may need to know things like how to operate the petty cash system, get photocopying done and answer enquiries.

Note down the most important office procedures that a new worker in your group would need to know.

Within the group

Communication within the management committee should be reasonably straightforward – if the committee is a good team you will be meeting regularly and talking informally between meetings. Communication within the rest of the group should also be straightforward if you all meet frequently (say, as a self-help group) and most members turn up. If you don't meet that often then you could consider:

- *A simple newsletter* – for which you need an editor good at twisting people's arms for contributions.

> Tuesday, 5th May   In : Lisa
>
> Phone messages :
>
> ✓① Lynn from Community Services wants another copy of our Annual Report — will deliver on my way home.
>
> ✓② Jason can't come to the training day on Saturday — Tariq informed
>
> ✓③ Exford garage. Van ready for collection. Les will collect.
>
> — Training Day — Dawn is doing the food. Tariq needs to know about arrangements for the key.
>
> ✱ Pauline : Can you ring Derek (611377) to find out then tell Tariq
>
> ✱ Also : Grant application forms are in Sarah's tray. She is coming in tomorrow (Wed). Can you make sure she sees them?

Fig. 7. Sample page from a Day Book.

- *Holding social gatherings* – so volunteers can get to know each other. Try combining these with fund-raising as one community radio group did – they organised gigs featuring local bands as a way of both getting members together and raising money to keep themselves going.

Example – breaking bread
Ruth who works with a counselling group believes that eating together

helps create bonds between people. Whenever her group meets for support or training sessions someone provides sandwiches while on special occasions everyone brings food and they all share a meal.

Keeping track of volunteers

In some groups volunteers go off on their own to visit people in their homes, or take calls on a helpline, or advise clients. You need some way of keeping track of all this activity so that you know not just what people are doing but how they are doing. What are the common problems? Are different people taking a different line in similar cases?

Volunteers working on their own need to report in regularly so they will feel supported and part of the group and you will be able to pick up on problems before they get serious. They need someone to report to – your volunteer co-ordinator if you have one, or if this is too much of a burden for one person, then perhaps a small volunteer support team who meet often. You should also set up regular meetings so volunteers can get together and exchange ideas and experiences.

Example – reporting back

The way one community mediation service gets its volunteer mediators to report back is to ask them to attend a debriefing session after every case. The mediators work in pairs helping people resolve disputes with their neighbours. In the debriefing sessions they have the opportunity to explore what went well and what less well in the case and to consider how successfully they operated as a pair. Any general problems that emerge from these sessions can be discussed with the rest of the mediators in the monthly support meeting or be brought to the management committee for further consideration.

With the outside world

For groups offering services, communication with users needs to be two-way. You need to let them know who you are and what you can offer. They need some means of letting you know whether they are satisfied with the service they receive.

Getting your group known can be a long drawn-out process. However many posters you put up, leaflets you give out, talks you give, fund-raising events you organise, there will never be any shortage of people who have never heard of you. Getting publicity is not the kind of task you can ever tick off as done. You just have to keep at it.

Getting feedback from users is easier. You can do this informally by asking them how they felt about the service they received and if there were any problems. Or more formally by using a simple evaluation form that asks them, for example, to rate the service (Very Good – Good – Satisfactory – Unsatisfactory), and pick out any aspects that were particularly helpful and any that could have been handled better.

KEEPING IN TOUCH WITH THE MEDIA

Local papers, radio and television are always on the lookout for stories about groups like yours. The operative word here is *stories*. The press don't just want to know you exist and do a good job, they need an angle: 'MP opens community cafe' – 'Hundredth case for new advice service' – 'Volunteers help toads across the road'.

To get your story to the attention of your local media you can ring their news desk and talk to a reporter and/or send them a press release. To put together a press release, use headed paper (Fig. 2 in Chapter 1 shows an example). Put 'PRESS RELEASE' at the top and the date then give your story a heading: 'Mayor to launch support group for young mothers'. Then tell your story remembering to:

- *Get over the main point in the first paragraph* – 'The Mayor of Newtown, Councillor Alan Brown, will launch a new support group for young mothers at the Allbury Community Centre on Tuesday 5 February at 10.30 a.m. Volunteers will offer practical help and friendship to young mothers who are isolated, bored and lonely.' Note that this paragraph tells the reader what will be happening, when, where, why and who will be there.

- *Make it personal* – include a relevant quote if you can: 'Mary Smith, co-ordinator of the new service, knows from experience that the group meets a real need: "I remember how I felt living in a tiny flat with no one to share things with. I thought the problems I was having with my son over feeding and potty training were just me," she says.'

- *Keep it short* – no more than one page.

- *Give a contact name and phone number* – where reporters can get further information.

If you haven't already done so, draw up a list of local media (with editors' names, addresses, phone numbers). Include local papers, paid for and free, local radio and TV, any community newsletters that are widely read. Use this list next time your group has a news story to sell.

Tips for dealing with the press

- *Give them a good story* – otherwise they may make one up for you. If you can provide a good photo-opportunity, so much the better.

- *Find a friendly reporter* – and talk to him or her regularly.

- *Don't fret too much if they get it wrong* – providing the story is not completely misleading. Most readers or listeners will only remember a few details. On the whole most publicity is good publicity.

PAYING EXPENSES

Why you should pay expenses

A recent survey of volunteers showed that one in three are sometimes out of pocket as a result of the work they do for free. Some large groups that could easily pay volunteers' expenses don't. There are two main reasons why your group should try to reimburse your volunteers:

- To make volunteering open to everybody. If you don't pay expenses you may be ruling out people on low incomes who can't afford to subsidise the group out of their own pockets.

- So you know how much your group really costs to run. If volunteers are carrying some of the load you can get a false picture.

If your group genuinely cannot afford to pay, you need to make this very clear to volunteers before they start.

ALLBURY COMMUNITY GROUP

EXPENSES CLAIM FORM

Name: **Period covered:**

Please give full details of expenses claimed and enclose receipt/ bill. For travel by car give mileage.

Date	Details of expenses	Amount
		Total_____

Signature_____

Authorised by _____

Please tick here if you wish to donate the amount claimed to the Group_____

Fig. 8. Example of an expenses claim form.

What you should pay

Your management committee will need to draw up a policy on expenses including:

- *Which expenses may be claimed* – for example: travel (to and from place of work and/or in the course of volunteering); postage; phone; meals on duty. You will need to set a mileage rate for volunteers who use their own cars.

- *How expenses should be claimed* – easiest if you design a claim form (see fig. 8).

- *Whether receipts need to be produced* – for everything or only for items over a certain sum?

When working out your policy two important principles to keep in mind are:

- *Pay volunteers for actual expenses they have incurred.* Any other method (for example, lump sum to cover expenses, monthly travel allowance) could lead to problems with the Benefits Agency or Inland Revenue.

- *Encourage everyone to claim the expenses they are entitled to.* This means you can get a realistic idea of the cost of your service. Make it easy for those who don't want the money to donate it back to the group (perhaps by ticking a box on the claim form).

Volunteer drivers

If your group uses volunteer drivers who do less than 4,000 miles a year they can claim their expenses at your group's ordinary mileage rate (provided the rate is not higher than Inland Revenue limits – currently 27p to 56p a mile depending on engine size). For drivers doing more than 4,000 miles a year the position is more complicated. Under Inland Revenue rules they must either accept a lower mileage rate over 4,000 miles or pay tax on their expenses. See the Volunteer Centre UK leaflet *Volunteers in the Driving Seat* for more details.

GETTING EVERYONE INSURED

If your group is hard-pressed you may feel insurance is a luxury you cannot really afford. In fact, insurance premiums are not an optional extra but part of your basic running costs like rent and phone. Broadly you need to think about insuring people, property and possibly vehicles.

People

You must have:

- *Employers Liability insurance* – if you employ any paid staff at all.

Compulsory under the Employers Liability (Compulsory Insurance) Act 1969, this covers you, as an employer, against claims for damages arising from the injury, death or illness of any employee.

● *Public Liability insurance* – also known as third party insurance. This provides cover for injury, loss or damage to anyone (including management committee members and volunteers) as a result of your group's negligence or failure to take adequate care.

You may also want to consider:

● *Trustee Liability insurance* – which gives management committee members some protection against personal liability in certain circumstances. You need to read the small print to check what is included. Only applies to registered charities.

● *Professional indemnity* – gives protection against giving wrongful information or advice. Worth thinking about if you run an information service or helpline.

Property
As with domestic insurance the main categories are:

● *Buildings* – if you rent an office your landlord will probably be responsible for insuring the building but double-check to make sure.

● *Contents* – you may have so little you are tempted not to bother. But think about the effect on your group if you have to replace, say, borrowed equipment. Equipment used away from your main headquarters may need extra cover.

Motoring
If your group owns any vehicles you will, naturally, already have them insured. If volunteers or paid staff use their own cars they should get confirmation in writing from their insurance companies that their normal domestic policy covers them for voluntary work. In most cases it will but a few insurers charge an extra premium.

Where to go for further advice
The NCVO has an excellent guide, *Insurance Protection – A Guide for*

Voluntary Organisations, which is well worth consulting. A few insurance companies have developed special schemes tailored to the voluntary sector. See the list of addresses at the end of the book for details.

CHECKLIST

The way you operate day-to-day will depend on the activities of your group. For many groups the main areas to think about are:

- *Co-ordinator* – do you need one? Paid or voluntary?
- *Tasks* – what are the main jobs that need doing in your group?
- *Equipment* – how to beg and borrow.
- *Health and safety* – how to stay on the right side of the law.
- *Paperwork* – is yours under control?
- *Communication* – within and outside the organisation.
- *Expenses* – and how to pay them.
- *Insurance* – which kinds do you need?

TALKING POINTS

- Is anyone in danger of burning out in your group?

- Does anyone (for example, funders) expect more of your group than you can give with the resources you have?

- What is the view of your group in the outside world?

5
How to Manage Money

Smaller organisations are so insecurely funded they often feel they might not be here in two years time.

(Michael Norton, Directory of Social Change)

Financial insecurity is a fact of life for many voluntary groups. Just because you've got a grant this year doesn't mean you'll automatically get one next year. Even if you do, your grant may be smaller. Or it may be bigger – it's the uncertainty that makes it so difficult to plan ahead.

Some groups do have secure funding – if yours is one of those you can skip the next few sections. Many more don't, however, and some exist on next to nothing. 'We had a tiny office with a studio we'd built ourselves,' says Karl who was the Treasurer of a local community radio group. 'But we never knew whether we were going to be able to pay the next quarter's rent. We always managed in the end – there'd be some frantic fund-raising and once someone gave us a big donation. But it got to be very wearing.'

Trying to run a group on too little money can take its toll and you need to be aware of this. Worrying about money – or the lack of it – can eat into your enthusiasm so the group sometimes feels like a weight hanging round your neck. In Karl's group the big expense was the rent – eventually they negotiated free premises in a local college which took off much of the pressure. Think about the big expenses in your group – is there any kind of deal you could make that would help to lighten the load?

HOW MUCH MONEY DO YOU NEED?

This is a 'how long is a piece of string' kind of question. The amount you need depends, partly at least, on the scale of your operations. Nikki's group, the AIDS helpline, are starting to think big now that they have three paid workers and their funding is fairly secure. 'What I'd really like is if we could have purpose-built premises on the ground floor. A drop-in centre – that's my dream.' Andrea's group, on the other hand – the one concerned with the needs of sick children – have scaled down their operations while they try to build up their pool of volunteers. They were left a legacy which should be enough to pay their modest running expenses until they are ready to expand their activities again.

Questions of scale

Here are some questions about scale for you and your co-organisers to mull over:

- *Can you avoid major expenses and still operate effectively?* For example, do you really need your own office? Will it stand empty and unused a lot of the time? Could you share?

- *Do you expect to expand, and if so, how quickly?* If you are thinking big from the start then you will have to look for big sources of funding. Salaries are a major expense so if you expect to employ paid staff in the near future you will need to be able to raise sizeable sums.

- *How much time and energy do you have for fund-raising?* This is a very important question. Raising money can be a time-consuming business while managing large sums is a big responsibility. Does your group want to give that much time? Take that much responsibility? Who in your group will actually do the fund-raising? Will the main activity be filling out forms to make grant applications, or organising fund-raising events? Have you got people willing to spend time in this way?

- *Could you handle large numbers of members?* Membership subscriptions are a good way of raising money especially in self-help or leisure groups. But members normally expect something in return for their subscriptions. Could you cope with large mailings? Chasing up people who don't renew?

Example – how to do a lot on a little money

Many groups achieve a lot on very little money. One local group of conservation volunteers which has been going for more than thirty years runs a year-round programme of conservation work including scrub clearing, fencing, bridging and coppicing. On a budget of around £2,500 a year they run a van (bought some years ago with a local authority grant), buy and maintain tools and safety equipment, insure volunteers and produce a quarterly newsletter. They have no staff, no office – the work programme is planned at weekly meetings in a room lent free of charge by Friends of the Earth.

LOOKING FOR FUNDING

Fund-raising is a major industry these days as the larger charities become more and more professional. One children's charity recently advertised for a full-time Trust and Research Officer to help in 'sustained efforts to raise income and support from charitable trusts.' If you hope to raise money for your group from grant-making trusts, these are the kinds of people you will be competing against.

Who gives what?

The point of saying this is not to make you disheartened. There certainly is money out there but the competition is fierce. To give you some idea of just how much is on offer:

- *Grant-making trusts and foundations* – give grants of over £900 million a year. Though over 2,500 are listed in the *Directory of Grant-Making Trusts* around two-thirds of the total comes from the top 300 trusts.

- *Local authorities* – have traditionally been a major source of voluntary group funding. Authorities in England give out over £600 million a year in grants and fee payments to locally based groups.

- *Central government departments* – gave nearly £500 million directly to voluntary organisations in 1991/2 mostly to national rather than local groups.

- *Companies – A Guide to Company Giving* looks at the contributions of nearly 1,500 firms. They gave around £270 million in 1991/2 in donations and community contributions (including sponsorship, loans of equipment, free premises, etc.).

- *European Social Fund* – allocated £25 million in 1993 mainly to employment projects.

Applying for funds

To get some of this cash flowing in your direction, start by getting hold of *Finding Funds*, a very useful National Council for Voluntary Organisations' publication which lays out all the options and tells you how to set about applying. If you don't know where to begin, think who might have a positive reason for being interested in your group's activities. For example:

- Nikki's group, the AIDS helpline, gets funding from their local health authority.

- Karl's community radio group got some money from their regional Arts Board.

- A community photography project approached film manufacturers for support with an exhibition and got a donation from Kodak.

- A training and support centre for women gets funding from their local authority and the European Social Fund.

Make a list of the most likely sources of funding for your group. If you have tried any sources already and failed, look again at your application. Is there anything you could have done better?

If you are intending to apply to trusts you could start by consulting FunderFinder, a computer program developed to help local groups identify the trusts most likely to fund them. Check whether your local Council for Voluntary Service or Rural Community Council has FunderFinder available.

Tips for applying for funds

- *Do some preliminary research.* Find out as much as you can about the trust or local authority department you are applying to. What are their policies, priorities, special interests? What kind of projects do they normally fund? How much do they give? Check application dates.

- *Take care over your application.* Once you know something about the funder you can tailor your application to suit them. Don't rush the forms at the last minute. Type your application if possible – and get names right. Argue your case as forcefully as you can making it clear how much you want and what you will use the money for. Imagine you were on the receiving end. Would you fund your group? Include supporting evidence – facts and figures showing what you've achieved so far. (See fig. 9 for a specimen letter to a local authority.)

● *Aim to build a relationship.* Don't be shy about contacting the council officers or trust staff who will be dealing with your application. They can be very helpful. If you are applying to a local authority find out which councillors are on the relevant committee and lobby them. Get them to see why it is important to your local community that they fund your group.

● *Remember to say thank you.* – if you are successful. And keep in touch by sending regular reports saying how the money is being used.

The 'contracts culture'

So far we have been talking about grants but for local authority funding in particular, times are changing. For groups providing services there has been a marked shift from straight grant-giving to service agreements and contracts. The relation between voluntary group and local authority is becoming one of purchaser/service-provider – with the added complication that the services provided may be liable to Value Added Tax (VAT).

If you enter into a service agreement with your local council you should seek expert advice on the wording of the contract and also check your VAT position. The National Council for Voluntary Organisations has some useful publications on contracts including a quarterly bulletin.

MANAGING YOUR MONEY

Members of management committees can sometimes be remarkably casual about money considering they can be held personally responsible if things go wrong. Some people switch off at the mere mention of finance preferring to leave it all to others. In fact, if your group is to manage its money effectively you all need to:

● *Take financial management very seriously* – most money messes are avoidable. They happen because nobody bothered to keep a close enough eye on what was going on.

```
ALLBURY DROP-IN CENTRE
Allbury Community Centre
45 Exford Road, Allbury AL6 9PZ
01777-633233


Mr G. Grant
Community Services Department
Allbury District Council
Town Hall
Allbury                                    30 September 199X


Dear Mr Grant,

COMMUNITY SERVICES GRANT
We should like to apply for a grant from the Community Services
Department. We enclose the completed application forms together
with our budget and a copy of our latest Annual Report.

As you will see from our application, the amount we are applying
for is significantly higher than last year. The main reason for the
rise is that we would like to be able to employ a part-time Project
Co-ordinator in the near future. The number of people using the
Centre has doubled over the past year (see statistics section, pages
12-14 of our Annual Report for detailed figures) and we have also
increased the number of advice sessions. If we are to develop the
Centre further we need the support of a paid worker.

If you need any further information, please let us know.

Yours sincerely,



I. Hope, Chair
```

Fig. 9. Letter to local authority applying for a grant.

- *Make sure you understand your group's financial situation* – and
  not just vaguely. Go through the figures. Ask your Treasurer questions. Persist until you have everything clear. Think out the impli-
  cations of making long-term commitments such as signing leases
  and discuss them. Consider what is the worst that could happen and
  how your group would cope.

- *Keep up-to-date* – make finance a regular item on management committee agendas. Get your Treasurer to give regular reports on the group's current financial situation.

- *Keep on top of the three Bs* – Budgeting, Bank Account and Book-keeping.

DRAWING UP A BUDGET

Though budgeting can seem complicated when you get into cash flow projections and capital v. running costs, the principles are actually very straightforward.

Your group's budget provides you with a basis for financial management. Before you have any money at all, drawing up a budget – that is, estimating all your costs and adding them all up – shows how much you will need to operate. For example:

Allbury Community Group
Estimate of expenses: 1 April 199x – 31 March 199y

Rent	1,500
Admin/Secretarial	800
Postage	250
Telephone	520
Publicity	300
Travel	130
Training	500
Insurance	250
Equipment	200
Miscellaneous	250
	4,700

If you are starting from scratch you may need to talk to another similar group to get a realistic estimate of what the various costs would be.

When you do have some income, setting this against your estimated expenditure shows whether you are likely to have a shortfall or a surplus:

Allbury Community Group
Estimated income

Members' subscriptions	1,250
Exford Trust	1,000
Donations	780
Fund-raising events	1,200
	4,230

You may want to have two columns – one for income which is certain, the other for money which is possible or probable.

On these figures this group is heading for a small deficit which may never materialise if their spending estimates are reasonably generous. What may be of more concern is cash flow – when during the year are they expecting their income to be paid? Will the money be there at the time they need it to pay rent or bills?

Look at the estimated income for your group – when do you expect the actual cheques? Look at your expenses – when do you expect your major bills? Will your income be there to cover them? If not, how are you going to manage?

Planning ahead

Your budget is an estimate but as the year goes by you will start to have actual figures for actual income and expenditure. By putting these alongside your budget figures you can monitor progress, see how far things are going according to plan. If you have not done so already, get together with your Treasurer and go through your budget noting down actual figures beside your estimates. Are there areas where your rate of spending is much higher or lower than expected? Should you be revising your budget?

Towards the end of the financial year you will have most of your actual figures which will show you how good your original estimates were – you will almost certainly have overestimated some kinds of expenditure and underestimated others. These actual figures will provide a basis for next year's budget adjusted for any changes you know are coming up.

Budgeting tips

- *Keep it simple.* One reason people don't engage with finance is that they don't understand what the figures mean. Try and keep your financial statements as simple as possible, with clear headings so everyone can follow.

- *Review often.* Be ready to revise your budget if a major change occurs such as unusual expenses or the unexpected loss or gain of a grant.

OPERATING A BANK ACCOUNT

When choosing where to open your account, the two main factors you need to consider are:

- *Charges.* Karl's group had free banking for several years before the manager wrote to say that, regretfully, the bank would be imposing charges in future. Unfortunately, the days of free banking for voluntary groups and charities are all but over. Some banks leave local managers some discretion but you will have to shop around. Though the distinction between banks and building societies is getting more and more blurred, with building society accounts you can normally avoid charges. However, depending on the type of account, you may not have a cheque book. If you don't, to pay money out you have to fill in a withdrawal form and take it to the building society who will issue the cheque.

- *Interest rates.* As well as a current-type account for day-to-day spending, you may also need a deposit-type account so that money you don't need immediately can be earning reasonable rates of interest. Check rates before you commit yourself so you get the best deal.

How many signatories?

When you open your account the bank or building society will normally ask for a copy of your constitution. You will also need to decide who may sign cheques (or withdrawal forms). Most groups name three or four signatories (including the Treasurer and often the Chair) and say cheques may be signed by any two of them. You need to be practical and choose people who can get together easily.

Banking tips

- *Keep cheque books and paying-in books in a safe place.*

- *Always fill in cheque book and paying-in book stubs.* Make a note on your paying-in book stubs of where the money came from, e.g. Exford Trust – 1st quarter.

- *Don't stockpile signed cheques.* Some Treasurers ask another signatory to sign a pile of blank cheques so they can use them when it is convenient. This may make the Treasurer's job easier but it removes the point of having two people to sign.

BASIC BOOK-KEEPING

Your group's 'books' are an accurate record of all the money paid in to your organisation and all the money paid out. If no one in your group has any experience of keeping financial records you should have a long talk with someone who does have the necessary expertise. The Community Accountancy Project book, *How to Manage your Money, If You Have Any*, can also get you off to a good start.

All groups need to keep proper accounts – for registered charities this is a legal requirement. Your Treasurer will keep records in what is called a cash book – the name can be confusing since most of the transactions may well be cheques and not cash at all. You can buy printed cash books in many sizes and formats.

Your cash book will have two parts (or you may choose to have two separate cash books): one to record money coming in, your income, the other to record money you pay out, your expenditure.

Cash received

The income side will have columns for Date, Details of who the cheque or cash came from, Receipt number (always issue a receipt and file a copy), and amount (headed Total). There will also be several Analysis columns so you can see clearly what different kinds of income you are receiving. These you would normally head, for example, Grants, Subscriptions, Events, Donations, etc.

When a cheque comes in your Treasurer will note the amount both in the Total column and in the relevant Analysis column. You may also want a column headed 'Bank' to note the amount banked at any one time – useful if you pay in several cheques at once since this will be the sum that corresponds with your bank statement.

Cash paid

The expenditure records will be organised similarly – columns for Date, Details, Cheque number, Amount paid out (Total), then Analysis columns with headings like the ones in your budget, for example: Rent, Admin, Postage, Telephone and so on, so you can see exactly what your money is being spent on (see fig. 10).

Check the Analysis columns in your cash book – are the headings the same as you have used in your budget?

Tips for keeping books

- *Always keep your books up-to-date.* Don't leave it till the end of the month to record transactions. Enter them as they occur – it should be possible at any time to look at the books and see your group's financial position.

- *Make sure you have a document for every transaction.* Give receipts for all money received and keep copies. Keep all invoices and receipts you get. Try and put all your transactions through the bank. If you are given cash, it is best not to spend it directly. Bank it first then pay out by cheque. For day-to-day spending of small sums, use petty cash (see below).

- *Check your bank statements against your cash book regularly.* Ask for monthly statements; make sure the entries are the same as in your cash book and the balance agrees.

Petty cash

'Petty cash' is not really petty at all. On the contrary, a workable petty cash system is crucial to the day-to-day running of your group. To set one up you need:

- *A petty cash box* – which could be a lockable cash box or a biscuit tin kept in a locked drawer.

Date	Details	Ref.	Total	Petty Cash	Rent	Admin	Post-age	Phone	Publi-city	Travel	Train-ing	Insur-ance	Equip-ment
199X May 2	Petty cash	183	50	50									
5	Allbury Council – rent	184	375		375								
10	British Telecom	185	103					103					
15	Exford Ink – printing	186	79						79				
23	Allbury CVS – copying	187	34			34							
25	M. Jones – expenses	188	6							6			
30	B. Swan – computer repair	189	53										53
	J. Dixon – expenses	190	12							12			
31	Petty cash	191	50	50									
			762	100	375	34	–	103	79	18	–	–	53

Fig. 10. Extract from a cash book: one month's payments, cash paid analysis.

101

- *A petty cash book* – where you record amounts of cash drawn from the bank as credits (these will appear in your Cash Paid book as Petty Cash) and all the different things the money is spent on – fares, stamps, coffee, etc. – as expenditure.

- *A petty cash file* – for receipts and petty cash vouchers (where there is no receipt) so that every item of spending has a document to go with it.

Tips for handling petty cash

- *Agree a maximum sum,* keeping in mind that too much cash around is a security risk.

- *Be clear who has responsibility for handling petty cash.*

- *Insist on a receipt or petty cash voucher* for every item of expenditure.

Annual accounts
Once a year your Treasurer will need to prepare a formal statement of your group's finances for the previous year. The simplest way to do these annual accounts is to produce a 'Receipts and Payments Account' which involves adding up all sums received and adding up all payments made (plus bank balance and cash in hand) and showing that the two totals match (see example on page 103).

A slightly more complicated version which gives a fuller picture of your group's position is an Income and Expenditure account accompanied by a Balance Sheet. If you are a registered charity you are required by law to produce accounts in this form. You should get help if you have not done this type of account before. See Further Reading section for guidance.

You will also need to get your accounts audited, that is, checked against your records by someone outside the group with experience of book-keeping. The auditor will add a statement to your accounts confirming that they give a true and fair view of your group's finances. The audited accounts would then be presented for approval at your Annual General Meeting. You don't need a professional accountant (unless you are a limited company). If you do use an accountant try and find one who will do the job for a minimal charge or for free.

Allbury Community Group
Statement of accounts, year ended 31 March 199y

Receipts

Cash in bank at 1.4.199x	38
Members' subscriptions	1,165
Exford Trust	1,000
Donations	780
Fund-raising events	825
	3,808

Payments

Rent	1,500
Admin/Secretarial	627
Postage	193
Telephone	432
Publicity	212
Travel	101
Training	200
Insurance	263
Equipment	52
Miscellaneous	108
Cash in bank at 31.3.199y	93
Cash in hand at 31.3.199y	27
	3,808

MAKING DECISIONS ON SPENDING

Your management committee is responsible for making sure your group spends its money wisely and in line with your constitution. 'People are only too ready to let everything through,' one Treasurer complained. 'I wish they would challenge me more – at least I'd feel they were interested.'

To spend money wisely you need to decide:

- *Who needs to spend money.* Try to keep it to as few people as possible. 'We were a bit lax sometimes,' Karl admits. 'People would order things nobody knew about till we got the bill.'

- *What do they need to spend it on.* Use your budget as the basis for organising spending. New ideas for spending not allowed for in the budget need to be discussed very carefully and approved by the whole management committee.

- *What authority do they need.* Groups sometimes set a modest sum below which spending by certain people does not require any further authority. Who will authorise higher spending? What criteria will they use?

RELATIONS WITH FUNDERS

Funders, especially local authorities, are taking more interest than perhaps they once did in the way their money is spent. You may, for example, find funders wanting to send a representative to your management committee meetings. If so, you should try and clarify their role. If they see themselves as there in a watchdog capacity how is that going to affect the running of your committee?

Not that funders taking a closer interest is necessarily a bad thing. Council officers can sometimes be extremely helpful and some have small contingency funds they can draw on to help you through a difficult patch. However, if you ever feel under pressure from funders to expand more quickly that you wish, for example, or take your group in directions you don't really want to go, then:

- *Talk to their officers – don't just moan.* If they have made any false assumptions about your group bring these out into the open and make the real position clear.

- *Remind them you are all (or nearly all) volunteers* – this does not bear on your professionalism but it may bear on the pace at which you can develop. Your group may get funding but as individuals you give your time and talents for free.

CHECKLIST

Money is nearly always an issue for voluntary groups. When managing money the main areas to think about are:

- *How much you need* – what is the scale of your operation?
- *Sources of funding* – which are the most likely for you?
- *Budgeting* – have you a firm basis for financial management?
- *Bank account* – are you getting the best deal?
- *Book-keeping* – are you keeping proper records?
- *Decisions on spending* – who needs to spend and on what?
- *Relations with funders* – how can these be most beneficial?

TALKING POINTS

- Why should anyone want to fund your group?

- What is the worst financial mistake your group has made?

- Suppose someone left your group a £20,000 legacy – how would you spend it? Suppose it was £10,000? £5,000?

6
How to Manage Everyone's Time

WHY TIME MANAGEMENT MATTERS

> I went into the office one morning last week to do the management committee minutes. Three hours later I'd barely started. One of the volunteers came in with her two-year-old to make an important phone call only she couldn't concentrate with Sam crawling all over her so I took him out . . . they'd only just gone when Sunil who manages the building popped in wanting to talk about photocopying then Bob arrived wanting a letter sent out – he can't use the word processor so I had to do it. And then it was the phone. . . Yellow Pages, did we want a bigger ad . . .
>
> (June, Secretary of a support group for
> people with mental health problems)

June tries to get into the office a couple of mornings a week but can't always manage it as she works part-time in a solicitor's office, has two school-age children and looks after an elderly neighbour as much as she can. Though her time is valuable, that morning the hours just melted away. She couldn't stay on to do the minutes because she had to get home, make lunch for her neighbour then get to work for 2.00 p.m. 'It's often like that,' June admits. 'I start something then someone comes in . . . the time just goes.'

Making the most of limited time

Managing time poses special problems in voluntary groups because everyone's time is so limited. June comes into the office for three hours twice a week if she's lucky. Less in the school holidays. She needs to use every moment to the full. Read the account of her morning again and see if you can think of ways she could use her time more effectively.

Here are some possibilities. June could try:

- Coming in earlier sometimes to take advantage of the quiet time first thing in the morning when she could expect fewer interruptions.

- Asking volunteers to come in only at specific times – say, after 11.00 a.m. so she would have uninterrupted time till then.

- Learning to say no. She didn't have to agree to talk to Sunil about photocopying just then. She could have said she was busy and offered another time, perhaps later in the morning or the next time she was in the office.

- Setting priorities – so she was clear in her own mind what she had to get done and what could wait. Could Bob's letter have been done another day, for example, or left for someone else to do?

HOW MUCH TIME CAN YOU EXPECT FROM VOLUNTEERS?

This is not a straightforward question in a voluntary group where people decide for themselves how much time they are willing to give. Normally the main organisers will give the most time – though precisely how much can prove a minefield. In one group both the Chair and Secretary had demanding full-time jobs so the time they could give was limited to some evenings and weekends. They felt they were doing their bit by producing a stream of bright ideas which they expected other organisers with more time to carry out.

Perfectly reasonable division of labour you might say – except that resentment began to build up as those with more time felt put upon. The Chair and Secretary always seemed to be giving orders. Why couldn't they do something themselves for a change? It wasn't long before the group was split by internal disputes.

If time is not to be a contentious issue, those with little time need to be tactful in asking others to do what they cannot do themselves. More generally, you need to:

- *Bring time problems into the open.* Talk about time before resentment builds up.

- *Don't take people who appear to have plenty of time for granted.* The decision on how much time to give is theirs not anyone else's. They could easily have other priorities that have nothing to do with the group.

Think about your group. How many hours a week does it take to run? Count all the hours you put in over a week and get your co-organisers to do the same. If you have any paid staff add in their hours. Does the total figure surprise you?

Paid staff
Taking on paid staff should take some time pressure off the main organisers. Your paid co-ordinator will do a fixed number of hours per week – though some go beyond the call of duty. One point to bear in mind is that your paid member of staff may not necessarily be any better than June at managing their time. They too may need help and guidance in making sure their hours don't simply melt away.

Volunteers
As well as volunteers running the group you may be recruiting other volunteers to provide the service you are offering in your community or to raise funds or help in some other way. Some of these volunteers may have lots of time to offer – a whole day or even more a week. Others may only have odd slots of time mainly in the evenings or at weekends.

Ideally you should try and use all the time you are offered. In practice this is not always easy since those with the most time may not be suitable for key posts while those with only the odd hour here and there may only know at the last minute they are free.

Attitudes to time
You may find it helpful to think of volunteers in terms of their attitudes to time. You may have volunteers with:

- *All the time in the world* – like Bob who took early retirement and volunteers partly to fill his time. When he came in wanting June to type his letter he wasn't in a hurry – this was his way of spending his morning. People like Bob can be very valuable precisely because they do have time. But they can also be infuriating to those trying to get things done quickly. One solution is to put people with all the time in the world in touch with one another. Find a specific project they might usefully do in a group of two or three making it clear who they should report to. If you take this route, make sure when the project is finished you use the results.

- *No time at all* – apparently, yet here they are volunteering. People like this can be valuable too because they can force the pace. If they attend a meeting they want to know what time it will finish and can we get on with the business please. You can use people like this for very specific tasks – phone x, y and z, find the names of the councillors on the community services committee. But it is usually best to get them working with others like themselves.

Example – keeping an eye on time

Volunteers' time commitment can easily change. Jobless people get jobs. Relatives fall ill and need looking after, suddenly depriving you of a key volunteer. Sometimes people with important roles try to hang on to them even when their circumstances change. Paul was unemployed when he got involved in Bob's group – the one that recycles donated furniture. He came in nearly every day and started calling himself the manager. After a few months Paul got a job in a local supermarket working late most evenings. He tried to keep up with the group but was getting tired trying to do two jobs at once. Only he was very reluctant to let go of either of them. When Bob tried to bring in another volunteer to help out – a retired woman with lots of time – Paul froze her out till she left in disgust. From being an asset Paul was becoming a problem – he couldn't do his job in the group properly any more but he wouldn't give it up.

What would you do if this was your group? Discuss the issue with your co-organisers.

SETTING PRIORITIES

One story has become a classic in the literature on time management. It features Charles Schwab, one-time president of Bethlehem Steel in the USA, and Ivy Lee, the consultant called in to show him how to make better use of his time. Not one for fancy theories, Lee merely handed his client a blank sheet of paper and told him to write down in order of importance his tasks for the next day. 'Tomorrow,' he said, 'start straight in on task no. 1. Keep going until it is finished, then go on to task no. 2. If a task takes you all day it doesn't matter so long as it's the most important one. If you don't get everything done, it's unlikely you could have done with any other system of doing things either.'

Lee did not charge for his advice. 'Try it,' he suggested, 'and when it works send me a cheque for what you think it's worth.' Schwab tried it. Bethlehem Steel prospered and Lee received a cheque for $25,000.

The moral of this tale is that managing time is mainly about working out priorities, learning to see the difference between what is essential and what is merely desirable. Though your group may be much more modest than Bethlehem Steel you still need to think about priorities:

- *For the group* – at your next management committee meeting list everything you need to achieve, or at least address, in the next three months – grant applications, open day, equal opportunities policy – then put them in order of importance.

- *For yourself* – whatever your role. There is a law that goes like this: 'A project carelessly prepared takes three times as long to complete as expected. A carefully planned one will only take twice as long.' In other words, everything takes more time than you think. However dedicated you are you will not achieve everything you hope to. This is a fact of life you have to live with so you need to be spending your time on the things that matter.

Keeping a time log

If you are like June – you feel pretty busy but time just seems to slip away – a good way to start sorting our priorities is to keep a time log to find out where your time is actually going.

Draw three columns on a piece of paper and head them: 'Time started', 'Activity' and 'Time taken' (see fig. 11). In the activity column write down absolutely everything you do during the time you are work-

Time started	Activity	Time taken
9.20	Arrive - Make coffee	5
9.25	Check Day Book	2
9.27	Ring Yasmin	12
9.39	Lunda with Sam	25
10.04	Start Minutes	5
10.09	Sunit - copying	20
10.29	Make coffee	5
10.34	Minutes	10
10.44	Post arrives - sort	10
10.54	Bob arrives - chat	15
11.09	Do Bob's letter	10
11.19	Call from Yasmin	15
11.34	Minutes	8
11.42	Call from Yellow Pages	6
11.48	Minutes	8
11.56	Call from CVS	10
12.06	Clearing up	5

Fig. 11. Time log based on June's morning.

ing for the group in the office or wherever. If you are a paid worker you may want to do this over two or three days.

Time logs nearly always throw up surprises. Did you really spend half an hour searching for that grant application form? And fifty minutes on the phone most of it chatting? Not that there is anything wrong with chatting but if you are only in the office for, say, three hours, fifty minutes is a big chunk of your time.

Now look at your time log and think about your priorities. What are you trying to achieve? Which activities help you achieve the results you want? Are you spending enough time on these activities, or too much on others that don't have all that much point?

Finally make another list – of things you need to do to achieve results. Are there tasks that don't appear on your time log? Could you do some of these next time you are in the office? But be realistic and think ahead. How, for instance, will you cope tactfully with interruptions?

Time management tips

- *Make lists* – putting jobs down on paper helps clear your mind and stops you worrying you'll forget something vital.

- *Be decisive* – if it's important, don't put it off. Do it now. Leave sharpening pencils and repotting plants till later.

- *Fix appointments to suit you* – don't assume you have to fall in with other people's plans.

- *Give yourself time to recharge* – be aware of your body rhythms. Go all out when you're fresh; ease off when you need a lift. And don't get anxious about time – do as much as you can and accept there are limits to what you can achieve.

LEARNING TO DELEGATE

Learning to delegate really means learning to trust other people to do things as well as you think you can. It means being prepared to accept they might do things better and they will almost certainly do them differently. If your group seems to be taking over your life, it may be that you are taking too much on yourself and need to let some things go. But how – in a group where no one has any real authority over anyone else?

Getting people to do things

Delegation has a special meaning in groups entirely run by volunteers where everyone is at the same level. You can't tell another volunteer to do something, but you can ask them. If they agree and you hand over a job you would otherwise have done yourself:

- *Be clear what has been agreed* – go over the details again trying to make sure there is no misunderstanding.

- *Agree a deadline.*

- *Monitor progress* – ask how it's going but in a spirit of encouragement not mistrust.

Sensitive areas

Letters can be a sensitive area especially in groups where all the people who know how to use the word processor are women, and those who don't know are men. Who types most of the correspondence in your group? Are you shoring up sexual stereotypes by assuming the women will do this kind of work? Could some of the men learn to use the word processor if someone spent a little time teaching them?

Sharing tasks

In a voluntary group delegating tasks should probably be translated into 'sharing the load'. People do get overloaded and they need to feel free to ask for help. Ways of spreading the load include:

- *Getting people working in groups* – so no one takes on too much on their own.

- *Creating more posts* (for example, press officer, social secretary, membership secretary) – so more people have smaller roles.

- *Brainstorming to find solutions to problems* – so problems are shared and no one feels they are carrying burdens alone.

PEOPLE WITH TIME PROBLEMS

Some kinds of people may have time problems. You need to look out for:

- *People who can't say no.* Are they being exploited by others who see them as an easy touch?

- *People who always take on more.* Watch for the phrase: 'I'll do it if no one else will'. They may do whatever it is but in a spirit of resignation which is good neither for them nor for the group.

- *Key figures, paid or not, who let the group take over all their waking hours.* They risk burning out and may need saving from themselves.

- *'Professional' volunteers* – people with their fingers in too many pies. Though they may have valuable experience such people are often most concerned with making your group slot into the tiny space they have created for it. Brian was one such volunteer who acted as press officer in one of his many groups. On one occasion he announced he was sending out a press release about an event not because it was the right time – it wasn't, it was two weeks too early

– but because he was going on holiday. It didn't matter that the press release would probably be ineffectual so long as it fitted in with his life.

- *Dreamers* – who take on tasks without the remotest idea how to carry them out. Only others don't know this until someone realises nothing is being done.

Tips for coping with other people's time problems

- *Check your assumptions* – don't always take what people say at face value – probe a little.

- *Help people say no* – if you suspect they are taking on too much.

- *Ask questions* – find out how people are doing before something goes badly wrong.

CHECKLIST

Managing time presents special problems in voluntary groups. The key areas you need to think about are:

- *Why time management matters* – the effects of each person having only limited time to give.
- *How much time to expect* – from organisers, paid staff, other volunteers.
- *Priorities* – why they matter and how to set them.
- *Delegating* – how to share the load.
- *People with time problems* – what to look out for.

TALKING POINTS

- What happens in your group when something needs doing urgently and nobody has time?

- Could your group use a volunteer with plenty of time to offer but needing lots of help and supervision?

- How easy do you find it to say no?

7
How to Cope With Common Problems

Running a voluntary group even moderately successfully is a major achievement when you think about it. There you are surviving mainly on goodwill, a shoestring budget, an unpaid workforce, no one having any real authority. Hardly surprising if you have problems occasionally.

All voluntary groups face problems sometimes, and most problems are caused by people. You may choose to believe your group is above organisational politics but you are almost certainly wrong. All groups have people pulling in different directions, bonds forming and unforming, strong characters determined to stick out for what they want, weaker characters ready to bend with the wind.

PLAYING PERSONALITY POLITICS

The worst thing you can do is bury your head in the sand and pretend that in your group all is sweetness and light. Conflict is both normal and healthy – provided it comes out into the open and is dealt with positively. To run your group effectively you need to be aware of who normally sides with whom, who wants what, who takes offence easily and who is as tough as old boots, who will always stick to their guns and who couldn't care less.

Every group has people liable to cause problems – here are just a few you might come up against:

The dominant character
There are some people everyone always listens to – whatever they say. Sandy was one of these – quick to react, definite, decisive: 'I don't agree with . . .' 'Why should we do that?' 'That's completely ridiculous.' Jeff took over as Chair of Sandy's group and at first he listened to Sandy too. Everyone did. Then he began to realise how destructive she could be, dismissing ideas out of hand and sometimes preventing proper

discussion. Her strength, he saw, lay in the force of her personality, not any special wisdom. Yet people still listened. Jeff was left wondering what to do. In the end he tackled the problem in three ways:

- *He got the measure of Sandy* – he observed, for example, that she was most destructive on matters she wasn't at all interested in like finance which bored her. He also realised she sometimes said the first thing that came into her head and could not back up her arguments.

- *He talked to Sandy* – about issues that were coming up and tried to get her on his side. She didn't always go along with him but she was less likely to be so negative.

- *He made a positive effort to take back control* – he took greater care to think out his own position on important issues. In meetings he began to argue back against Sandy and force her to defend her views.

Do you have a Sandy figure in your group? How do you handle him or her?

The powerful clique

Seventeen-year-old Becky joined a community arts group – she was attracted to one of the project groups that made radio programmes. They were all young people around her age and she went along a couple of times but soon dropped out. 'They all seemed to know each other,' she explained when she ran into the organiser a few weeks later. 'They made you feel stupid if you didn't know how to use the equipment.'

Some sub-groups build up a strong team spirit which is good for insiders – but the downside can be that they feel cliquey and unwelcoming to those who don't belong. It is difficult to dilute the power of cliques, but you can try:

- *Treating each member as an individual* – taking them aside, talking to them separately, asking one of them to take on particular responsibilities such as looking after a newcomer like Becky.

- *Injecting a strong character into the group* – someone like Sandy who would stir things up.

- *Limiting their power to take action* – making sure they are not in a position to hijack the group, taking it off in a direction no one else has agreed.

Does your group have powerful cliques? How do they operate and how do you cope?

The wayward soul

Some people will always go their own way however hard you try to keep them on the same track as everybody else. They dance to different music – which is fine until they cause havoc in your group by sending out a press release no one knows about or committing the group to something you don't want to do.

Lawrence had been the driving force behind his group when it was being set up. In the early days he was a one-man-band, free to act as he thought fit, but now the group was underway with an elected management committee he was causing problems by taking things into his own hands. Lawrence did not appreciate anyone trying to interfere with what he did. He felt as one of the founders he was special and anyway, he always had the interests of the group at heart. If anyone complained he acted hurt that people did not seem to appreciate the hard work he had put in at the start. Lawrence's management committee tried various approaches including:

- *Keeping in close touch* – ringing him often so they had plenty of warning of what he was up to.

- *Making more effort* – to make him feel all his early work was appreciated.

- *Inviting him to do specific tasks* – the idea was to bring Lawrence into the fold, but the effect was actually to drive him away. Lawrence, it became clear, was one of those people who like the excitement of setting up something new – he just wasn't interested in the ordinary, mundane business of keeping the group going. Asked to do specific tasks he made excuses. He began to lose interest and eventually turned his attention to a fresh cause.

Do you have a Lawrence figure in your group? What is the effect and how do you cope?

What kind of political animal are you?

Simon Baddeley and Kim James are psychologists interested in organisational politics. They start from the assumption that everyone in an organisation adopts some kind of political behaviour – burying your head in the sand is just as 'political' as lobbying.

In their view, the way any one individual behaves politically stems from two types of skill: skill in understanding or reading the external world and skill in managing their own desires, feelings and emotions. To make these ideas more concrete they have described four types of political behaviour symbolised by four animals. In your group you may be politically:

- *A sheep.* Sheep-like political behaviour is very common and arises from a combination of political unawareness and personal integrity. Political sheep hate the whole idea of politics and are disturbed when they find power exercised from sources such as ambition or personality. To them this seems wrong – they judge all politically aware people as just out for themselves.

- *A donkey.* Political donkeys are simply inept – like sheep but without the personal integrity, they simply have no idea what makes other people tick.

- *A fox.* Very politically aware but out for their own ends, foxes are clever and good at manipulating others to get what they want. Sheep think all politically aware people are foxes.

- *An owl.* Political owls are the most effective animals since they combine political awareness with personal integrity. They are wise enough to be able to read an organisation, understand where power lies and how decisions are arrived at. They are balanced enough emotionally to use this political awareness in a positive way.

Think about the political animals in your group. Who are the sheep, the foxes and the owls? Have you any political donkeys?

EXPECTING TOO MUCH

Problems sometimes arise in voluntary groups because busy organisers expect too much of volunteers. Not everyone is dynamic, self-motivated and full of initiative. Many people are perfectly competent if they get guidance and support, but if they are thrown in at the deep end, they flounder.

Running a group staffed by volunteers is not the same as running an organisation with a paid workforce. Volunteers do not normally compete for jobs. They offer their time and if they appear reasonably suited and their references do not throw up any problems, their offer is accepted. As an organiser you can certainly look for people with particular experience and skills but you may not find them. In that case you simply have to do your best with the people you've got.

Learning on the job

Fortunately volunteers are often very flexible, willing to have a go at things they have never tried before. When someone shows willing like this, you need to take into account that they are learning and not expect everything to be perfect first time round. Kate offered to be press officer for her group. She had never done anything like this before but she was outgoing and a quick learner and worked hard at her first assignment – getting publicity for a fund-raising event. She was pleased when the local paper carried the story though the article was a bit misleading. When the organisers saw the piece they complained loudly about the mistakes it contained making Kate feel they thought it was her fault. It didn't occur to anyone to think that, with no experience of press or publicity, she had done very well to get coverage at all. No one said well done, she felt discouraged and her confidence sagged.

Getting people to give their best

People can often do wonders but nine times out of ten they don't because no one gives them the support and encouragement they need. To help people produce their best you need to:

- *Make use of individual strengths.* Find out what people enjoy and are best at. Work with their abilities.

- *Recognise inexperience.* If people are doing something for the first time make sure they get encouragement, help and guidance.

- *Build up confidence.* Don't knock it down like the organisers of Kate's group.

- *Celebrate success.* People like to feel good. If something is well done, don't just take it for granted, say so loud and clear so everyone can hear.

COPING WITH PEOPLE WHO WHINGE

When you are doing your best and working flat out to keep your group afloat, there's nothing worse than people who whinge – 'No one told me . . .' 'I didn't like the way . . .' 'Why aren't we . . .?' You can be forgiven for harbouring black thoughts against whingers. Don't they realise all the hard work going on?

The fact is they probably don't realise. People who whinge are most often on the fringes of a group with little idea what is happening at the centre. One way to cut down on their whinging is to try and involve them more.

Looking on the bright side

You may find this difficult to believe but there is a positive side to whinging. Having a good moan is one of the ways people give feedback in organisations. If someone moans to you, you should be pleased – it shows you are in touch and that people tell you things rather than complaining behind your back. Most whinges do actually have a grain of truth in them – taking them on board is a way of showing the troops you are taking notice of what they say.

A difficult lesson

People feel free to whinge when they think 'someone ought to be doing something'. But who? It can be very hard to get across that in a group run entirely, or almost entirely, by volunteers, there is no 'someone' out there. The group is no more and no less than its members. You may need to find a tactful way of suggesting to constant complainers that the 'someone who ought to be doing something' could easily be themselves.

Tips for dealing with whingeing

- *Look for ways of raising morale in the group* – could you organise social occasions, celebrations, public events?

- *Work at team building* – is everyone keen to get away as quickly as possible after meetings? Could you spend more time together, perhaps go to the pub?

- *Take whingers seriously* – but not too seriously. Try and take action if there is a real problem but don't let them give you sleepless nights.

WHEN SOMEONE MAKES A MISTAKE

The Treasurer of one group received an invoice for some advertising he knew nothing about. 'Oh yes, I was going to mention that,' said one of the publicity group. 'It was when you were away – they were offering us a good rate only I had to give them an answer straightaway. I had a word with Cath – she thought it was a really good deal.' 'But Cath's not on the finance committee,' the Treasurer protested, 'and anyway, we can't afford it.' It was pointless arguing though – he knew the group had no alternative but to pay.

Things like this happen in voluntary groups – people take decisions without authority or show bad judgement or send out letters that offend. It can be difficult to avoid mistakes with volunteers doing things in their own time and key people not always around.

Clearing up the mess

If mistakes do happen you need to act quickly:

- *Find out what happened.* Talk to the people involved, keeping in mind that there are at least two sides to most stories.

- *Deal with any damage outside the group.* Make any necessary apologies immediately.

- *Don't dwell on who is to blame.* People who have messed up usually feel bad even if they are brazening it out.

- *Learn from what happened.* Look for ways of making sure the same thing doesn't happen again. The Treasurer stuck with paying for advertising his group could ill afford realised that the procedures for authorising spending were in urgent need of tightening up.

Dealing with complaints

If your group offers services to the public you need to consider how you would handle a complaint from one of your users. Best not to wait till it actually happens. Work out a policy for dealing with complaints including:

- who people should complain to;
- what the group will do to investigate complaints and how soon;
- what kinds of action may be taken to deal with complaints.

You also need to think how you would deal with a complaint against a volunteer. How would you investigate it? What kinds of behaviour would be serious enough for you to dismiss a volunteer? What if a volunteer has a problem with the group or another volunteer – who should they complain to? Some groups have a formal grievance procedure dealing with such issues. The Volunteer Centre UK booklet *Volunteers First* includes a sample grievance procedure to use as a starting point.

LOSING SUPPORT

'All voluntary groups have peaks and troughs . . . if a key person leaves, for example, the heart can drop out of things for a while,' says Andrea, Chair of the group concerned with the needs of sick children. Starting a new group can be much easier than keeping a long-standing group going. Some groups are crying out for an injection of new blood. The same people do the same jobs year after year – not necessarily because they want to but because no one else is willing to take over.

You can soon end up in a vicious circle. If your organisers are tired, their enthusiasm muted, this shows in the atmosphere. New people sense the cloud hanging over the group, the desperation to hand over the reins – they take fright and don't come back. So the organisers get even more tired, their enthusiasm even more muted . . .

Weathering troughs

If your group is going through a bad patch, you may need to:

- *Ask searching questions.* Why has the group lost support? Has it outlived its usefulness? Is it time for a change of direction?

- *Make a big splash.* You can try very hard to shake off your tired image. Organise a big event perhaps by teaming up with another group in a similar field. Start a recruitment drive – work out exactly what you want newcomers to do. Think about what you can offer – if you were an outsider would you join your group? If not, why not? What might make you change your mind?

- *Scale down your activities.* If you can't manage a big splash then you may have to reduce your workload to manageable proportions. Accept your limitations and don't feel guilty about not doing more.

Example – the hospital box

Andrea's group did a recruitment drive which produced several new volunteers. Though it was too early to ask the newcomers to take on key roles, Andrea made sure they became active immediately. One of the group's activities is to lend out 'hospital boxes' to playgroups and schools to prepare children for being in hospital. Two of the new volunteers agreed to work together taking responsibility for the boxes. Andrea also encouraged them to come up with new ideas for the way they were used.

CHECKLIST

All groups face problems at some time or another. When coping with problems the key areas to think about are:

- *Personality politics* – who are the owls, sheep, foxes and donkeys?
- *Expecting too much* – do your volunteers need more help and support?
- *Whingers* – can you involve them more?
- *Mistakes* – can you limit the damage?
- *Losing support* – are you being realistic?

TALKING POINTS

- What is the worst problem you have dealt with while running your group?

- How good is your group at dealing with conflict?

- How does your group deal with complaints?

8
Fixing the Legal Framework

When Karl agreed to be Treasurer of his local community radio group he never really thought much about the legal side of things. As he saw it his main responsibility was to keep the books efficiently – which he did. 'It was only when we got a licence to do a temporary broadcast and had some legal training that it really came out how we were an unincorporated association and we could be personally liable if things went wrong. People suddenly started saying – but what about libel? What would happen if somebody decided to sue us?'

Karl is not particularly unusual in his lack of awareness about the legal structure of his group. People setting up voluntary groups are normally fired with enthusiasm for an interest or cause. Questions like 'How do we stand in the eyes of the law if someone wants to sue us or we can't pay our bills?' come way down the list of concerns.

Unfortunately, however, 'I'd never thought about it' or 'I didn't realise' are not acceptable excuses if things do go wrong. If you are involved in running a voluntary group it is important to have key legal concepts clear.

UNDERSTANDING YOUR LEGAL STRUCTURE

The distinction Karl's group were not properly aware of is one we touched on in Chapter 2: the difference between a group being **incorporated** and **unincorporated**. If you don't know which your group is, the odds are you are unincorporated. You have to take positive steps to become incorporated whereas many people run unincorporated groups blissfully unaware of their status.

Groups which are unincorporated
If your group is neither a company limited by guarantee nor an industrial and provident society – the two main forms of incorporation open to voluntary groups – then you are almost certainly unincorporated. For

most purposes a group which is unincorporated is, in the eyes of the law, simply a collection of individuals who get together to pursue a common aim. Such groups may have various legal structures the most common being:

- *An unincorporated association (or society or club) governed by a constitution.* Such groups often have a membership structure and are democratically run. Like Allbury Community Group – set up after a public meeting with members who pay £5 a year to join, run by a management committee called the Executive Committee which is elected by members at the Annual General Meeting.

- *A trust.* This structure is only suitable for voluntary groups with charitable aims. Trusts have existed since time immemorial normally to manage money or property for some clearly defined purpose. Setting up a trust creates a formal relation between three parties: the donor of the money or property, the trustees who nominally own the money or property, and the beneficiaries. Groups with a trust structure are less democratic. Normally their activities are governed by a legal document called a trust deed which names a small number of trustees who take responsibility for all the decision-making.

The significant point in law about unincorporated groups whatever their legal structure is that the group itself has no separate legal existence. Anything the group wants to do has to be done by individuals (normally members of the management committee or trustees) acting on the group's behalf.

This is where the vexed question of liability comes in – if the group has no separate existence then technically the group cannot run up debts or be sued. If things go wrong, the buck stops with the people running the group. They may be held personally responsible as individuals for the group's obligations and debts.

That is the downside of being unincorporated. The reality is not as bad as it sounds. Thousands of groups have operated for long periods as unincorporated associations or charitable trusts and lived to tell the tale. Some risks such as giving bad advice are insurable against. Trustee liability insurance can lessen the risk for those running registered charities. The important thing is to be aware of your unincorporated status so you can plan accordingly and not be taken by surprise.

Groups which are incorporated

Incorporated associations do have a legal existence of their own. Groups which incorporate – that is, become a company limited by guarantee or an industrial and provident society – can hold property and enter into contracts and employ staff in their own name. This is the first main advantage.

The second is that incorporation limits to some degree the personal liability of the people running the group. If your group were to incorporate by becoming a company limited by guarantee, this would mean that members guarantee to pay a nominal sum (say, £1–£5) towards any deficit that may arise if the company were to be wound up. The extent of anyone's personal liability is limited to the nominal sum they guarantee.

It is important to note, though, that the people running the group are not entirely freed from personal liability. They may still be held responsible for breaches of trust, for example, or continuing to run the company when insolvency is clearly looming.

The downside of being a limited company is that legal fees can make registration expensive, while once you are registered you will be subject to more red tape than before since you now have to comply with company law (in addition to charity law if you are registered as a charity).

Should you incorporate?

If the question arises in your group two important factors to consider are:

- *Scale*. Groups often think about incorporating as they expand and start employing staff or entering into contracts. The switch in local authority funding from straight grants to contracts has made some groups consider taking this step.

- *Risk*. What risks does your group face? Is personal liability really an issue? List the main risks your group and the people running it are exposed to. How real are they? Can you insure against them? Would incorporation make a difference?

If you are considering incorporation, the golden rule is to seek legal advice early. Groups differ in their individual circumstances. You need expert help to work out what is best for you. For more details on legal structure, see *Voluntary but not Amateur* (London Voluntary Service

Council) and also *Charitable Status: A Practical Handbook* by Andrew Phillips, both listed in the Further Reading section at the end of this book. Andrew Phillips' book is also very useful when considering the issues raised by the next section.

DECIDING WHETHER TO REGISTER AS A CHARITY

The question of legal structure – whether you are an unincorporated association or a charitable trust or a company limited by guarantee – is quite separate from the question of charitable status.

People are sometimes confused about what it means to register as a charity – which is perhaps not surprising when groups such as the Chartered Institute of Journalists which don't sound particularly charitable are registered while groups such as Amnesty International which do seem charitable are not. Some people feel that charity law needs to be radically overhauled but until it is the rules for registration remain broadly as they have been for many years.

As things stand your group may register as a charity, whatever its legal structure, if you can satisfy the Charity Commissioners that all the aims and objectives laid out in the 'Objects' clause of your constitution are charitable in their definition of the term.

Do you have charitable aims?
Their definition of charity dates back to Elizabethan times. To register your activities must fall into one of four categories sometimes known as the 'four heads of charity':

- the relief of the poor, the handicapped and the aged;
- the advancement of religion;
- the advancement of education;
- other purposes beneficial to the community.

Though it may appear that this last category could cover almost any good cause, the Commission will need to be convinced that your group's activities bring some genuine benefit not just to a small group of people but to a substantial part of the community.

Are you obliged to register?
There is no absolutely straightforward answer to this question. 'The Chair of one group came to see me,' said a local solicitor who often advises voluntary groups. 'He said we've been going since 1988 and we

were wondering if we should apply for charitable status. I said is your income more than £1,000? "Oh yes," he said. I told him you have no choice.'

The solicitor gave this response because he knew that a group should register with the Charity Commission if what they do falls under one of the 'four heads of charity' and one of the following apply:

- the group has a total income over £1,000;
- they use or occupy land including buildings, e.g. have an office;
- they have a permanent endowment (that is, property which cannot be spent as income).

In fact, there is no sanction for not registering. And furthermore, it is the Charity Commission and not the group that has the final say on whether the group has charitable aims and may register as a charity. So the fact that you think you should register doesn't necessarily mean the Charity Commission will agree. For more detail see the Charity Commission booklet *Starting a Charity*.

Advantages of charitable status

The main advantages to groups of charitable status are:

- *Financial* – including exemptions from most forms of direct taxation.

- *Status and credibility* – a charity registration number is seen as a stamp of approval reassuring funders and other supporters that you are genuine and respectable. Some funders have a policy of only grant-aiding registered charities.

Disadvantages

There are also some disadvantages, the main ones being:

- Political and campaigning activity is strictly limited.

- Trading activity is also limited.

- Your group is subject to monitoring by the Charity Commission and must comply with charity law – including submitting annual accounts and stating on all official documents that your group is a registered charity.

APPLYING FOR CHARITABLE STATUS

You need to be prepared for registering as a charity to take a long time – from several months to as long as two years in some cases. One group described the process as 'very tortuous' but that was a few years ago. More recently the Charity Commission has taken steps to make the process of registration simpler.

Model governing documents
One way it has tried to make life easier for groups is by producing draft model governing documents for:

● the constitution of an unincorporated association (see Appendix);

● a trust deed;

● a Memorandum and Articles of Association (the governing document of a company limited by guarantee).

Groups are not obliged to use these models but registration is made simpler if they do. The model documents are available free of charge from the Charity Commission. If you already have a constitution (or a trust deed or Memorandum and Articles of Association) you may still find it useful to get hold of the relevant model to compare it with your own.

Starter pack
If you want, or think you are required to, register as a charity the first step is to contact the Charity Commission who will send you a starter pack. As well as an explanatory booklet the pack contains a very detailed questionnaire which all groups wanting to register must fill out. The aim is to sort out early questions such as whether the group's activities really do fall into one of the four charitable categories.

The Commission asks to see a copy of your governing document at this point. If your group is still at the setting-up stage you should send in your draft constitution before it is formally adopted.

Registration
The Commissioners use the information in the questionnaire to see whether any changes are necessary to your group's governing document before you can qualify as a charity. Only when they are satisfied that

your group's activities are charitable and have agreed the form of your group's governing document do they ask you to complete a formal application to register.

Once registered your group gets a charity registration number which you need to show on all official documents. There is currently no charge for registration.

KEEPING ON THE RIGHT SIDE OF THE LAW

If you are a self-help group with minimal income meeting monthly in someone's front room your activities are barely touched on by the law. But if you run an office, or register as a charity, or employ someone even for only a few hours a week, the law will start to impinge. Below is a list of some of the main areas of legislation that can affect voluntary groups. Which ones affect you?

Legal checklist

- *Charity law* – if you are registered as a charity. The Charities Act 1992 tightened up on the way charities are managed. Not all the provisions of the Act are yet in force. The Charities Act 1993 was a consolidating Act bringing together existing charity law dating back to 1872.

- *Health and safety laws* – if you employ staff/have premises/engage in physical activity. The Health and Safety at Work Act is the main legislation to concern you (see Chapter 4).

- *Employment laws* – if you employ staff. As well as health and safety laws you will also need to be familiar with the Employers Liability (Compulsory Insurance) Act 1969 (see Chapter 4) and the Employment Protection (Consolidation) Act 1978 amended by various Employment Acts which deal with contracts of employment, rights and conditions of service (see Chapter 9). Other legislation which can affect employing people includes the Equal Pay Act 1970, the Sex Discrimination Act 1975 and the Race Relations Act 1976.

- *Company law* – if you are a limited company. If you do incorporate, your company directors and any staff will need access to expert advice on how to comply with current company law.

- *Tax laws.* If you are a registered charity you will be exempt from most direct taxation. If you trade you will need to check your Value Added Tax (VAT) position with Customs and Excise.

- *Children Act* – if you work with children. The National Council for Voluntary Child Care Organisations is a good starting point for information on the requirements of the Act.

- *Data Protection Act* – if you hold information about people on computer. (see Chapter 2).

CHECKLIST

To operate effectively you need to know where you stand in the eyes of the law. The main areas to consider are:

- *Incorporated or unincorporated* – are you clear about the difference?

- *Charitable status* – should you register as a charity?

- *Applying to the Charity Commission* – how it works.

- *Where does your group stand* – which areas of the law affect your group?

TALKING POINTS

- Do you think voluntary groups are subject to too much red tape?

- Are there ways your group is not complying with the law?

- How easy does your group find it to get good legal advice?

9
How to Employ Staff

DECIDING WHETHER TO EMPLOY STAFF

Geoff was the first paid worker to be employed by a local Community Association: 'When I met people from the management committee at the interview I had the impression they were active and pretty dynamic. But once I took over the job I hardly saw them. They just seemed to melt away.'

Running a group when you're all volunteers can be hard work, harder perhaps than any of you imagined. Some groups are only too keen to hand over the reins to paid staff as soon as they can raise the funds. If your group is looking to take on paid staff it is important to remember:

- *It's still your group.* Even if you do employ one or more workers, the management committee still has ultimate responsibility for everything the group does.

- *Staff need support and supervision.* You shouldn't expect them just to get on with it. Geoff's management committee didn't take their responsibilities as employers seriously. They left him largely to his own devices – which in his case wasn't too disastrous since he was able and resourceful. Not all groups are so lucky.

Do you really need staff?
If the answer seems blindingly obvious, that may be because you are concentrating only on the positive side of employing staff. There certainly are significant advantages including:

- *Smoother running.* Your organisation is less at the mercy of crises in volunteers' personal lives. Your group can be 'open for business' more days of the week.

- *More opportunities for development.* When Jackie took over as paid co-ordinator of a victim support scheme the group was struggling along with a handful of volunteers able to respond only to the most urgent calls. With the injection of her time and energy the number of volunteers increased to fifty and the group is able to respond to nearly every call.

- *Better public image.* In some eyes, paid staff give an organisation extra credibility.

But there are also disadvantages such as:

- *More responsibility.* The management committee will have to take on a new role, that of employer. Certain officers, usually the Chair and the Treasurer, will have extra work.

- *More funding needed.* The cost of employing even one part-time worker can be significant. Once you take someone on, you will need to keep the funds rolling in so you can continue to pay their salary. This can lead to worry if you rely on grants since the amount of your grant will vary from year to year.

- *Possible loss of control.* This may happen if too much authority is handed over to paid staff, or if the management committee operates at arms length.

Note down the advantages you think paid staff would bring to your group. Now list the disadvantages. How do the two lists compare?

WRITING JOB DESCRIPTIONS

When groups first think about employing staff they often have no more than a hazy notion of what they want the person to do. Usually the idea is that the staff member will 'run things'. That's what Geoff's management committee thought.

Unfortunately this is not good enough. Before you recruit anybody you need to work out what the job you are offering actually consists of. We talked about 'job descriptions' and 'person specifications' for volunteers in Chapter 3. You need to go through the same procedure for paid staff only more so. List the tasks and areas of work you want the person to be responsible for as the basis for drawing up a job description. Think about the skills and qualities you will be looking for in the person who does the job.

Drawing up a job description helps concentrate the mind. Normally you would send a version to people applying for the job as well as to those you ask to provide references. Job descriptions usually include:

- *Job title* – such as Volunteer Co-ordinator, Project Worker, Administrator.
- *Employer* – the name of your group.
- *Location* – the place or places the employee would work.
- *Who the person is responsible to* – in the case of one worker, this would normally be the management committee.
- *Hours* – is the job full or part-time? How many hours per week?
- *Duties* – be realistic here, you may not be able to include all the tasks on your list especially if your worker is only part-time. You will need to decide which are the priority areas.

(See the example in fig. 12.)

FINDING THE RIGHT PERSON

You can get an idea of suitable salary rates from looking at adverts in your local paper. Some groups use the salary scales (and also conditions of service) of larger organisations such as local authorities. When you are working out how much it is going to cost your group to employ a worker don't forget to include the costs of recruiting, such as advertising the post and paying travelling expenses of people you interview. If equal opportunities are to mean anything in your group you need to make positive efforts to attract as wide a range of applicants as possible. That means advertising the job widely – through newspaper adverts (expensive unfortunately), local radio (they may have a job spot), Job Centres and anywhere else you can think of (see fig. 13).

Once the closing date has passed you will need to:

- *Draw up a shortlist* – look at experience and qualifications together with the overall impression of the person that comes over from their application.

- *Take up references* – preferably before the interviews. Otherwise you can only offer the job provisionally subject to satisfactory references.

ALLBURY COMMUNITY GROUP
DROP-IN CENTRE PROJECT

JOB DESCRIPTION
PROJECT CO-ORDINATOR

Job Title: Project Co-ordinator

Employer: Allbury Community Group

Location: Allbury Drop-In Centre, Exford Road, Allbury

Hours: Full-time (35 hours per week including some
                   evening work)

Responsible to: Executive Committee, Allbury Community Group

DUTIES
To be involved in the day-to-day running of the Allbury Drop-In
Centre for unemployed people including:

- Answering the telephone and dealing with enquiries

- Explaining to new users how the Centre operates

- Co-ordinating the work of volunteer staff

- Liaising with other agencies concerned with the needs of unemployed people

- Contributing to the development of the Centre

Conditions of service: as laid down in the enclosed documents

Fig. 12. Example of a job description for a paid worker.

- *Set up interviews* – giving candidates at least a week's notice.
  Decide who will conduct the interviews. Get together and agree
  between you what skills and qualities you are looking for and the
  kinds of questions you will ask.

135

```
┌─────────────────────────────────────────────────────┐
│                                                       │
│         The 99 Allbury Avenue Neighbourhood Project   │
│                    has a vacancy for a                │
│                                                       │
│                    PROJECT WORKER                     │
│              (18 hours per week: £7,059)              │
│                                                       │
│                                                       │
│             To develop new programmes of work with    │
│                10-14-year-old children and to contribute to │
│         the general running of this successful neighbourhood project. │
│                                                       │
│      We are looking for someone with experience of working with │
│      children of this age-group and commitment to community projects. │
│             Office administration skills also required. │
│                                                       │
│           For a job description and application form, contact │
│           Jill O'Brien, Neighbourhood Project, 99 Allbury Avenue, │
│                        Allbury AL9 2AL                │
│                        01777-644266                   │
│                                                       │
│                 Closing date: July 15th 199X          │
│          We positively welcome applications from all sections │
│                       of the community                │
│                                                       │
└─────────────────────────────────────────────────────┘
```

Fig. 13. Example of a job advertisement.

Interviewing for the job

Jackie was not impressed by the way she was interviewed for her co-or-dinator's job. 'I was going to be working on my own from home. They should have been trying to find out – is this person going to have the persistence to stick at what we want them to do when there isn't anyone to provide the working atmosphere? They didn't do that at all.' Jackie got the job anyway – and did it well. Like Geoff's group, hers too were lucky.

As we noted in Chapter 3, it is not easy to interview well. Look back to the tips given there for interviewing volunteers. Much of the advice holds true for interviewing paid staff too. You need to ask plenty of open questions, get the candidates doing most of the talking. Press them for concrete evidence of things they've done in the past, paid or volun-tary, that show how they will cope with the job you need them to do. Try and assess whether they are positively interested in your group's work. What efforts have they made to find out more about you?

When it comes to deciding who should be offered the job, don't just go on gut feeling. List the pros and cons of each candidate to help you select the most suitable. That way you will be clear why you chose one and not another.

YOUR RESPONSIBILITIES AS AN EMPLOYER

Taking on staff means your management committee taking on a whole new area of responsibility. Before taking the plunge and becoming an employer you need to talk to someone with employment experience – a personnel officer in your local council, perhaps – to get advice on what you need to know as well as the pitfalls to avoid. These are the main new areas you will need to become familiar with:

- *Contracts of employment.* The law requires you to give employees a written statement of their terms and conditions of service. It is good practice to give all employees, full or part-time, a contract of employment as soon as they start work. You should always seek legal advice on drawing up a contract. The process will make you aware of the various rights employees have in law (see the Department of Employment booklet PL716 *Individual Rights of Employees* for a summary) and make you consider questions such as holiday entitlement, sick pay and pensions. The contract should also give details of your disciplinary and grievance procedures (see below).

- *Employers Liability insurance.* This is required under the Employers Liability (Compulsory Insurance) Act. See the section on insurance in Chapter 4.

- *PAYE and National Insurance.* Employees are entitled by law to individual, detailed written pay statements – you can buy pre-printed pay slips in office stationers. Your Treasurer will need to master the basics of PAYE and National Insurance since you will be responsible for deducting tax and National Insurance contributions from your employee's pay as well as paying an employer's National Insurance contribution. The Community Accountancy Project book *How To Manage Your Money, If You Have Any* has a short section on PAYE to get you started.

The Department of Employment has free booklets on most aspects of employing staff. ACAS also produces useful publications.

SUPERVISING STAFF

Remember Sam from Chapter 2? He was the co-ordinator of a group for visually impaired people who got very little supervision and support from his management committee but preferred it this way to having, as he saw it, the committee 'breathing down his neck'.

Paid staff often have mixed feelings about the volunteer management committees who are technically their employers responsible for managing their work. The relationship can be successful but only if you decide right from the start:

- *Who is responsible for supervising staff.* In Jackie's case one of the management committee sits in the office with her regularly to discuss her work. She is appreciative: 'The sessions quite often throw up good ideas such as a random sample questionnaire about our service.' If no one on your management committee has any experience of managing, you may need to look for someone else to take on the role.

- *How much authority the staff member should have.* You need to make it clear what kinds of decisions your paid worker can make on their own and what kinds need consultation – and with whom. Generally decisions that bear on policy should be referred to the management committee. But for this to work someone – the Chair or the person responsible for supervision – needs to be available by phone for consultation.

Tips for managing staff

- *Keep in touch* – don't let staff spend long periods without any contact from the management committee. Remember too that a solitary worker can become very isolated.

- *Look out for problems* – don't wait for trouble to erupt. Take active steps to find out how things are going.

- *Build in regular reviews* – set aside time once or twice a year to talk to your staff member about their work, how they are doing, how they see the future and any training you or they feel they need.

- *Don't ignore conflict* – which may brew up between staff and volunteers, for example, or between staff and a member of the management committee, or among staff if you have more than one worker. Try and nip problems in the bud.

- *Remember: personality matters* – and will come to matter more the more staff you take on. In one group with several staff what started as minor personality differences between two people escalated to the point where the group closed down for a month and three people left.

COPING WITH CHANGE

Whatever else it does, taking on paid staff will most certainly bring change as members of the management committee and other volunteers take less responsibility for the day-to-day running of the group. The paid staff will gradually become the main point of contact and the best informed about everyday concerns. For this to be a change for the good, you need to think back to the second golden rule:

- **Don't take anything for granted**

To achieve a fruitful partnership between management committee and paid staff, each partner needs to explain themselves clearly to the other. Both sides need to check assumptions, bring differences into the open. Right from the start.

Paid staff and volunteers

The transition from everyone being a volunteer to one or more paid workers and the rest volunteers has to be handled carefully. In one group volunteers had been accustomed to doing everything themselves for several years. Then they employed a co-ordinator who found life difficult in the early days: 'Volunteers had been used to coming in in their lunch hour to send letters to clients. They'd grab the computer and I'd be left with nothing to do. They found it hard to hand over that kind of work.'

The most successful paid workers are often people who are also volunteers themselves in other groups – they know how it feels to be a volunteer and are less likely to create a feeling of 'them and us' or tread on sensitive toes.

Tips to avoid tension

● Take positive steps to make volunteers feel they are still valued.

● Make sure your paid worker is clear how their role relates to that of the volunteers.

DEALING WITH PROBLEMS

Discipline and grievances

In Chapter 7 we suggested you might find it useful to work out a formal grievance procedure to help cope with problems and complaints. If you employ paid staff a clear disciplinary and grievance procedure becomes a must. You need to have thought out and written down what steps would be taken if the behaviour of a member of staff or their performance in the job was unsatisfactory. They need to know what to do if they have a grievance against you.

You should try and keep your procedures simple and fair. ACAS has a Code of Practice: 'Disciplinary Practice and Procedures in Employment', a copy of which can be found in the Department of Employment booklet *Individual Rights of Employees* (PL716).

Keep in mind when dealing with problems that in employment law following the right procedure can be as important as the merits of the case.

Redundancy

It may seem odd before you have even taken anyone on to think about redundancy – but given that uncertain funding is often a fact of life for voluntary groups, the possibility that you may not always have the money to pay a worker needs to be faced. The Department of Employment has booklets on aspects of redundancy including your responsibilities and employees' rights.

ENDING ON A POSITIVE NOTE

In the end, as your group starts to take off, you probably will want to employ staff. Just make sure you do it at the right time and in the right way. Start as you mean to go on – put the relationship on a proper footing. Remember – voluntary is not amateur. And the very best of luck.

CHECKLIST

Sooner or later you will consider employing paid staff. The main areas to consider are:

- *Making the decision* – do you really need paid staff?
- *Job descriptions* – what do you want the person to do?
- *Interviews* – how to find the right person.
- *Responsibilities* – as an employer.
- *Supervision* – who is going to manage your staff?
- *Change* – making the transition painless.
- *Problems* – the importance of observing the correct procedures.

TALKING POINTS

- If you were a paid worker how would you feel about being managed by volunteers?

- Think about voluntary groups you know – those with paid workers and those without. What are the key differences?

- What has given you the most satisfaction in running your group – and what has given the most frustration?

Appendix

DRAFT CONSTITUTION FOR AN UNINCORPORATED ASSOCIATION

This draft is based on a model draft governing document (Booklet GD3 'Model Constitution for a Charitable Unincorporated Association') issued by the Charity Commission to groups wishing to register as a charity. Please note that this draft is included here for information only. **If you wish to use it as a basis for your constitution you must get hold of Booklet GD3 from the Charity Commission.**

CONSTITUTION

adopted on the . . . . day of 19

A. Name
The name of the Association
is . . . .('the Charity')

B. Administration
Subject to the matters set out below the Charity and its property shall be administered and managed in accordance with this constitution by the members of the Executive Committee, constituted by clause. . . . .of this constitution ('the Executive Committee').

C. Objects
The Charity's objects ('the objects') are . . . .
. . . .
. . . .

D. Powers

In furtherance of the objects but not otherwise the Executive
Committee may exercise the following powers [*you would include only
those powers relevant to your group*]:

- power to raise funds and to invite and receive contributions
  provided that in raising funds the Executive Committee shall not
  undertake any substantial permanent trading activities and shall
  conform to any relevant requirements of the law;
- power to buy, take on lease or in exchange any property necessary
  for the achievement of the objects and to maintain and equip it for
  use;
- power subject to any consents required by law to sell, lease or
  dispose of all or any part of the property of the Charity;
- power subject to any consents required by law to borrow money
  and to charge all or any part of the property of the Charity with
  repayment of the money so borrowed;
- power to employ such staff (who shall not be members of the
  Executive Committee) as are necessary for the proper pursuit of
  the objects and to make all reasonable and necessary provision for
  the payment of pensions and superannuation for staff and their
  dependants;
- power to co-operate with other charities, voluntary bodies and
  statutory authorities operating in furtherance of the objects or of
  similar charitable purposes and to exchange information and
  advice with them:
- power to establish or support any charitable trusts, associations or
  institutions formed for all or any of the objects;
- power to appoint and constitute such advisory committees as the
  Executive Committee may think fit;
- power to do all such other lawful things as are necessary for the
  achievement of the objects.

E. Membership [*for groups whose members will all be individuals*]

1 Membership of the Charity shall be open to any person over the age
of 18 years interested in furthering the objects and who has paid the
annual subscription laid down from time to time by the Executive
Committee.

2 Every member shall have one vote.

3 The Executive Committee may by unanimous vote and for good reason terminate the membership of any individual: Provided that the individual concerned shall have the right to be heard by the Executive Committee, accompanied by a friend, before a final decision is made.

F. Membership (alternative)
Charity Commission model contains an alternative clause for charities who will have as members organisations as well as individual members.

G. Honorary Officers
At the annual general meeting of the Charity the members shall elect from amongst themselves a chairman, a secretary and a treasurer, who shall hold office from the conclusion of that meeting.

H. Executive Committee
1 The Executive Committee shall consist of not less than.......members nor more than ....members being:
> (a)   the honorary officers specified in the preceding clause;
> (b)   not less than......and not more than......members elected at the annual general meeting who shall hold office from the conclusion of that meeting. *[Charity Commission model contains a clause (c) on members nominated by specific organisations]*

2 The Executive Committee may in addition appoint not more than.......co-opted members but so that no-one may be appointed as a co-opted member if, as a result, more than one third of the members of the Executive Committee would be co-opted members. Each appointment of a co-opted member shall be made at a special meeting of the Executive Committee called under clause.....and shall take effect from the end of that meeting unless the appointment is to fill a place which has not then been vacated in which case the appointment shall run from the date when the post becomes vacant.

3 All the members of the Executive Committee shall retire from office together at the end of the annual general meeting next after the date on which they came into office but they may be re-elected or re-appointed.

4 The proceedings of the Executive Committee shall not be invalidated by any vacancy among their number or by any failure to appoint or any defect in the appointment or qualification of a member.

5 Nobody shall be appointed as a member of the Executive Committee who is aged under 18 or who would if appointed be disqualified under the provisions of the following clause.

6 No person shall be entitled to act as a member of the Executive Committee whether on a first or on any subsequent entry into office until after signing in the minute book of the Executive Committee a declaration of acceptance and of willingness to act in the trusts of the Charity.

I Determination of Membership of the Executive Committee
A member of the Executive Committee shall cease to hold office if he or she:

1 is disqualified from acting as a member of the Executive Committee by virtue of section 45 of the Charities Act 1992 (or any statutory re-enactment or modification of that provision);

2 becomes incapable by reason of mental disorder, illness or injury of managing and administering his or her own affairs;

3 is absent without the permission of the Executive Committee from all their meetings held within a period of six months and the Executive Committee resolve that his or her office be vacated; or

4 notifies to the Executive Committee a wish to resign (but only if at least three members of the Executive Committee will remain in office when the notice of resignation is to take effect).

J Executive Committee Members not to be personally interested
No member of the Executive Committee shall acquire any interest in property belonging to the Charity (otherwise than as a trustee for the Charity) or receive remuneration or be interested (otherwise than as a member of the Executive Committee) in any contract entered into by the Executive Committee.

[Model includes further clause covering cases where the Executive Committee needs to include a professional person who will charge a fee for their services.]

K Meetings and proceedings of the Executive Committee
1 The Executive Committee shall hold at least two ordinary meetings each year. A special meeting may be called at any time by the chairman or by any two members of the Executive Committee upon not less than 4 days' notice being given to the other members of the Executive Committee of the matters to be discussed but if the matters

include an appointment of a co-opted member then not less than 21 days' notice must be given.

2 The chairman shall act as chairman at meetings of the Executive Committee. If the chairman is absent from any meeting, the members of the Executive Committee present shall choose one of their number to be chairman of the meeting before any other business is transacted.

3 There shall be a quorum when at least one third of the number of members of the Executive Committee for the time being or three members of the Executive Committee, whichever is the greater, are present at the meeting.

4 Every matter shall be determined by a majority of votes of the members of the Executive Committee present and voting on the question but in the case of equality of votes the chairman of the meeting shall have a second or casting vote.

5 The Executive Committee shall keep minutes, in books kept for the purpose, of the proceedings at meetings of the Executive Committee and any sub-committee.

6 The Executive Committee may from time to time make and alter rules for the conduct of their business, the summoning and conduct of their meetings and the custody of documents. No rule may be made which is inconsistent with this constitution.

7 The Executive Committee may appoint one or more sub-committees consisting of three or more members of the Executive Committee for the purpose of making any inquiry or supervising or performing any function or duty which in the opinion of the Executive Committee would be more conveniently undertaken or carried out by a sub-committee: provided that all acts and proceedings of any such sub-committees shall be fully and promptly reported to the Executive Committee.

L   Receipts and expenditure
1 The funds of the Charity, including all donations contributions and bequests, shall be paid into an account operated by the Executive Committee in the name of the Charity at such bank as the Executive Committee shall from time to time decide. All cheques drawn on the account must be signed by at least two members of the Executive Committee.

2 The funds belonging to the Charity shall be applied only in furthering the objects.

M Property

1 Subject to the provisions of sub-clause 2 of this clause, the Executive Committee shall cause the title to:

— all land held by or in trust for the charity which is not vested in the Official Custodian for Charities; and

— all investments held on behalf of the charity;

to be vested either in a corporation entitled to act as custodian trustee or in not less than three individuals appointed by them as holding trustees. Holding trustees may be removed by the Executive Committee at their pleasure and shall act in accordance with the lawful directions of the Executive Committee. Provided they act only in accordance with the lawful directions of the Executive Committee, the holding trustees shall not be liable for the acts and defaults of its members.

2 If a corporation entitled to act as custodian trustee has not been appointed to hold the property of the charity, the Executive Committee may permit any investments held by or in trust for the charity to be held in the name of a clearing bank, trust corporation or any stockbroking company which is a member of the International Stock Exchange (or any subsidiary of any such stockbroking company) as nominee for the Executive Committee, and pay such a nominee reasonable and proper remuneration for acting as such.

N Accounts

The Executive Committee shall comply with their obligations under the Charities Act 1992 (or any statutory re-enactment or modification of that Act) with regard to:

1 the keeping of accounting records for the Charity;

2 the preparation of annual statements of account for the Charity;

3 the auditing or independent examination of the statements of account of the Charity; and

4 the transmission of the statements of account of the Charity to the Commissioners.

O Annual Report
The Executive Committee shall comply with their obligations under the Charities Act 1992 (or any statutory re-enactment or modifications of that Act) with regard to the preparation of an annual report and its transmission to the Commissioners.

P Annual Return
The Executive Committee shall comply with their obligations under the Charities Act 1992 (or any statutory re-enactment or modification of that Act) with regard to the preparation of an annual return and its transmission to the Commissioners.

Q Annual General Meeting
1 There shall be an annual general meeting of the Charity which shall be held in the month of. . . . . in each year or as soon as practicable thereafter.

2 Every annual general meeting shall be called by the Executive Committee. The secretary shall give at least 21 days' notice of the annual general meeting to all the members of the Charity. All members of the Charity shall be entitled to attend and vote at the meeting.

3 Before any other business is transacted at the first annual general meeting the persons present shall appoint a chairman of the meeting. The chairman shall be the chairman of subsequent annual general meetings, but if he or she is not present, before any other business is transacted, the persons present shall appoint a chairman of the meeting.

4 The Executive Committee shall present to each annual general meeting the report and accounts of the Charity for the preceding year.

5 Nominations for election to the Executive Committee must be made by members of the Charity in writing and must be in the hands of the secretary of the Executive Committee at least 14 days before the annual general meeting. Should nominations exceed vacancies, election shall be by ballot.

R Special General Meetings
The Executive Committee may call a special general meeting of the Charity at any time. If at least ten members request such a meeting in writing stating the business to be considered the secretary shall call such a meeting. At least 21 days' notice must be given. The notice must state the business to be discussed.

S Procedure at General Meetings
1 The secretary or other person specially appointed by the Executive Committee shall keep a full record of proceedings at every general meeting of the Charity.

2 There shall be a quorum when at least one tenth of the number of members of the Charity for the time being or ten members of the Charity, whichever is the greater, are present at any general meeting.

T Notices
Any notice required to be served on any member of the Charity shall be in writing and shall be served by the secretary or the Executive Committee on any member either personally or by sending it through the post in a prepaid letter addressed to such member at his or her last known address in the United Kingdom, and any letter so sent shall be deemed to have been received within 10 days of posting.

U Alterations to the Constitution
1 Subject to the following provisions of this clause the Constitution may be altered by a resolution passed by not less than two thirds of the members present and voting at a general meeting. The notice of the general meeting must include notice of the resolution, setting out the terms of the alteration proposed.

2 No amendment may be made to clause. . . . .(the name of the charity clause), clause. . . . .(the objects clause), clause. . . . .(Executive Committee members not to be personally interested clause), clause. . . . .(the dissolution clause) or this clause without the prior consent in writing of the Commissioners.

3 No amendment may be made which would have the effect of making the Charity cease to be a charity at law.

4. The Executive Committee should promptly send to the Commissioners a copy of any amendment made under this clause.

V Dissolution
If the Executive Committee decides that it is necessary or advisable to dissolve the Charity it shall call a meeting of all members of the Charity, of which not less than 21 days' notice (stating the terms of the resolution to be proposed) shall be given. If the proposal is confirmed by a two-thirds majority of those present and voting the Executive

Committee shall have power to realise any assets held by or on behalf of the Charity. Any assets remaining after the satisfaction of any proper debts and liabilities shall be given or transferred to such other charitable institution or institutions having objects similar to the objects of the Charity as the members of the Charity may determine or failing that shall be applied for some other charitable purpose. A copy of the statement of accounts, or account and statement, for the final accounting period of the Charity must be sent to the Commissioners.

W   Arrangements until first Annual General Meeting
Until the first annual general meeting takes place this constitution shall take effect as if references in it to the Executive Committee were references to the persons who signatures appear at the bottom of this document.

This constitution was adopted on the date mentioned above by the persons whose signatures appear at the bottom of this document.

Signed . . . .

Useful Addresses

MAIN ORGANISATIONS OFFERING HELP AND ADVICE TO VOLUNTARY GROUPS

Community Matters, 8/9 Upper Street, London N1 0PQ. Tel: 0171-226 0189.

Directory of Social Change, Radius Works, Back Lane, London NW3 1HL. Tel: 0171-284 4364.

National Council for Voluntary Organisations, Regent's Wharf, 8 All Saints Street, London N1 9RL. Tel: 0171-713 6161. Trustee Helpline: 0171-833 1818.

The Volunteer Centre UK, Carriage Row, 183 Eversholt Street, London NW1 1BU. Tel: 0171-388 9888.

OTHER USEFUL ADDRESSES

Action with Communities in Rural England (ACRE), Somerford Court, Somerford Road, Cirencester, Glos GL7 1TW. Tel: 01285-653477. (For details of Rural Community Councils.)

Advisory, Conciliation and Arbitration Service (ACAS) (London Region), Clifton House, 83–117 Euston Road, London NW1 2RB. Tel: 0171-396 0022. (ACAS has a network of regional offices.)

Association of Charitable Foundations (ACF), High Holborn House, 52–54 High Holborn, London WC1V 6RL. Tel: 0171-404 1338.

Bradford Council for Voluntary Service, 19–25 Sunbridge Road, Bradford BD1 2AY. Tel: 01274-722772. (For information on health and safety.)

Charities Aid Foundation, 48 Pembury Road, Tonbridge, Kent TN9 2JD. Tel: 01732-771333.

Charity Commission, St Alban's House, 57–60 Haymarket, London SW1Y 4QX. Tel: 0171-210 4477.

Community Accountancy Project, The Print House, 18 Ashwin Street, London E8 3BL. Tel: 0171-249 7109.

Community Service Volunteers, 237 Pentonville Road, London N1 9NJ. Tel: 0171-278 6601.

FunderFinder, 65 Raglan Road, Leeds LS2 9DZ. Tel: 0113-2433008.

London Voluntary Service Council, 356 Holloway Road, London N7 6PA. Tel: 0171-700 8107.

National Association of Councils for Voluntary Service, 3rd Floor, Arundel Court, 177 Arundel Street, Sheffield S1 2NU. Tel: 0114-2786636.

National Association of Volunteer Bureaux, St Peter's College, College Road, Saltley, Birmingham B8 3TE. Tel: 0121-327 0265.

National Council for Voluntary Child Care Organisations, Unit 4, Pride Court, 80–82 White Lion Street, London N1 9PF. Tel: 0171-833 3319.

Northern Ireland Volunteer Development Agency, 70–74 Ann Street, Belfast BT1 4EH. Tel: 01232-236100.

Office of the Data Protection Registrar, Wycliffe House, Water Lane, Wilmslow, Cheshire SK9 5AF. Tel: 01625-535777.

REACH, Bear Wharf, 27 Bankside, London SE1 9DP. Tel: 0171-928 0452.

Volunteer Development Scotland, 80 Murray Place, Stirling SK8 2BX. Tel: 01786-479593.

Wales Council for Voluntary Action, Llys Ifor, Crescent Road, Caerphili CF8 1XL. Tel: 01222-869224.

FOR DETAILS OF INSURANCE SCHEMES FOR VOLUNTARY AND CHARITABLE ORGANISATIONS

Alexander & Alexander (UK) Ltd, 65/71 London Road, Redhill, Surrey RH1 1YN. Tel: 01727-774177.

CTS Ltd (Trading branch of Community Matters), 8/9 Upper Street, London N1 0PQ. Tel: 0171-354 9569 or 01273-813121.

Further Reading

To browse through the range of books and booklets available ask these organisations for an up-to-date list of their publications (see Useful Addresses):

- Community Matters

- Directory of Social Change

- National Council for Voluntary Organisations (NCVO)

- The Volunteer Centre UK

- Charity Commission – leaflet CC1 gives a list of their leaflets

Below are some suggestions for further reading.

GENERAL

The Good Trustee Guide (A4 ring binder), edited by Kate Kirkland, NCVO, 1994.
Just About Managing, Sandy Adirondack, London Voluntary Service Council, 2nd edition, 1992.
Voluntary but not Amateur, Duncan Forbes, Ruth Hayes and Jacki Reason, London Voluntary Service Council, 3rd edition, 1990.
Making Charities Effective, A Guide for Charities and Voluntary Bodies, Peter L. George, Jessica Kingsley Publishers, 1989.
Essential Volunteer Management, Richard Lynch and Steven McCurley, Directory of Social Change, 1994.
Running a Charity, Francesca Quint, Jordans, 1994.
Getting Organised: A Handbook for Non-Statutory Organisations, Shirley Otto and Christine Holloway, NCVO Publications, 1985.

On Trust – Increasing the Effectiveness of Charity Trustees and Management Committees, NCVO Publications, 1992.
Croner's Management of Voluntary Organisations, Croner Publications (loose-leaf reference service with quarterly updates).
Understanding Voluntary Organisations, Charles Handy, Penguin, 1988.
'Owl, Fox, Donkey or Sheep: Political Skills for Managers', Simon Baddeley and Kim James, *Management Education and Development*, Vol. 18, 1987.

FINANCE

Charitable Status: A Practical Handbook, Andrew Phillips, Directory of Social Change, 4th edition, 1994.
Organising Your Finance: A Guide to Good Practice, NCVO Publications, 1987.
Insurance Protection: A Guide for Voluntary Organisations, NCVO Publications, 1992.
Getting Ready for Contracts: A Guide for Voluntary Organisations, Sandy Adirondack and Richard Macfarlane, Directory of Social Change, 2nd edition, 1993.
Finding Funds, NVCO Publications, 2nd edition, 1993.
A Guide to Company Giving, ed. Michael Eastwood, Directory of Social Change.
A Guide to the Major Trusts, (2 vols), Directory of Social Change.
Directory of Grantmaking Trusts, Charities Aid Foundation.
How to Manage Your Money, If You Have Any, 3rd edition, Community Accountancy Project, available from Community Matters.
A Practical Guide to PAYE for Charities, Kate Sayer, Directory of Social Change, 1994.

BOOKLETS

Making the Right Choice, Angela Whitcher, The Volunteer Centre UK, 3rd edition, 1992.
All Expenses Paid, Angela Whitcher, The Volunteer Centre UK, revised edition, 1992.
Volunteers in the Driving Seat: A Practical Guide for Volunteer Drivers, Ruth Horton, The Volunteer Centre UK, new edition, 1993.

Volunteers First, The Personnel Responsibilities of People who Manage Volunteers, Angie McDonough and Angela Whitcher, The Volunteer Centre UK, 1991.

Trustee Liability Insurance – Is It For You? NCVO Publications, 1993.

Employing People: the ACAS Handbook for Small Firms, available from Community Matters or ACAS.

JOURNALS

NCVO News published 10 times a year by the National Council for Voluntary Organisations, Regent's Wharf, 8 All Saints Street, London N1 9RL. Annual subscription £25 for voluntary groups.

Third Sector published 24 times a year by Third Sector, 4 Assam Street, London E1 7QS. Tel: 0171-247 0066. Annual subscription £30.

Voluntary Voice published 10 times a year by the London Voluntary Service Council, 356 Holloway Road, London N7 6PA. Annual subscription £25 for voluntary groups.

Volunteers published 10 times a year by The Volunteer Centre UK, Carriage Row, 183 Eversholt Street, London NW1 1BU. Annual subscription £20.

Community, published quarterly by Community Matters, 8/9 Upper Street, London N1 0PQ. Annual subscription £5.

VIDEOS

It's for Charity – explains the work of the Charity Commission, available on free loan from the London office of the Charity Commission.

Charity Trustees – the 'Crucial' Guide to Trusteeship, with Lenny Henry, available free to groups from the London office of the Charity Commission.

Also look out for: *Voluntary Sector Television – BBC Select*, 2nd Monday/Tuesday night of each month.

Glossary

AGM: Annual General Meeting. Yearly meeting of a group where accounts are formally approved and officers and committee members elected.

constitution: document laying out the rules for running an organisation.

co-opt: invite someone on to a committee by agreement of the other members.

co-ordinator: name often given to the main worker, paid or unpaid, in a voluntary group.

Council for Voluntary Service: local voluntary organisation set up and run by local voluntary groups to promote and develop the work of the voluntary sector in their area.

data protection: data protection laws require anyone holding information about people on computer to register with the Data Protection Registrar. The law also allows people to have access to information held about them on computer.

employee: person who works directly in return for wages and for whom a contract of employment exists.

general meeting: meeting open to all members of an organisation.

holding trustees: people who hold the assets and investments of a charity for safe keeping. Not to be confused with the trustees who manage the organisation.

management committee: term often used to describe the committee or board with legal responsibility for a voluntary group and everything it does.

members: people who have applied for and been granted membership of an organisation. In groups with a membership structure members are entitled to vote at general meetings including the AGM.

minutes: formal written record of the business conducted at a meeting.

press release: written statement issued to the press normally to try and get media coverage for a story or event.

quorum: minimum number of people who must be present at a meeting for any decisions taken to be valid.

registered charity: a voluntary organisation registered with the Charity Commission and having a charity number.

Rural Community Councils: independent charities working to promote the welfare of rural communities by encouraging community self-help, local initiatives and voluntary effort. RCCs offer advice and practical help.

trustee: a person responsible for the overall management and control of a charity.

unincorporated association: term used to describe the legal structure of a group of people who get together for a common purpose and draw up a constitution or rules to govern the way their activities will be run.

user: person who makes use of the services of a voluntary group.

voluntary group or organisation: an organisation managed by a voluntary body known as the management committee (or board or some similar name) which has legal responsibility for its activities. It may or may not be a registered charity.

voluntary sector: difficult to define precisely. Consists of a wide range of organisations and informal groups from small community and self-help groups to large, international organisations such as Oxfam.

volunteer: person who willingly works for the good of others outside their immediate family not directly in return for wages.

Index

159

160 Index